WeightWatchers®

Eat! Move! Play!

A word about Weight Watchers

Weight Watchers International, Inc. is the world's leading provider of weight-management services, operating globally through a network of company-owned and franchise operations. Weight Watchers holds more than 48,000 weekly meetings, where members receive group support and education about healthful eating patterns, behavior modification, and physical activity.

Weight-loss and weight-management results vary by individual. We recommend that you attend Weight Watchers meetings to benefit from the supportive environment you'll find there and follow the comprehensive Weight Watchers program, which includes food plans, an activity plan, and a thinking-skills plan. In addition, Weight Watchers offers a wide range of products, publications, and programs for those interested in weight loss and weight control.

For the Weight Watchers meeting nearest you, call 800-651-6000. For information on bringing Weight Watchers to your workplace, call 800-8AT-WORK. Also, visit us at our website, WeightWatchers.com, or look for *Weight Watchers Magazine* at your newsstand or in your meeting room.

WeightWatchers®

Eat! Move! Play!

A Parent's Guide for Raising Healthy, Happy Kids

WILEY

JOHN WILEY & SONS, INC.

Published by John Wiley & Sons, Inc., Hoboken, New Jersey

Published simultaneously in Canada

LIBRARY OF CONGRESS CATALOGING-IN-PUBLICATION DATA

Weight Watchers eat! move! play! : a parent's guide for raising healthy, happy kids.
   p. cm.
  Includes index.
  ISBN 978-0-470-47420-4 (pbk.)
  1. Children--Nutriiton. 2. Parenting. I. Weight Watchers International.
  RJ206.W365 2009
  649'.1--dc22
                          2009020806

Manufactured in the United States of America

10 9 8 7 6 5 4 3 2 1

acknowledgments

When Weight Watchers decided to create a book to help parents deal with the countless issues that come up when they're trying to raise and feed their children in a healthy way, we began by seeking out a team of talented and creative individuals who were passionate about this topic. In fact, when people heard about *Eat! Move! Play!*, the typical response was, "This book needs to be done!" or "It's perfect that Weight Watchers is doing this book." Their enthusiasm and hard work translated into what we feel is the definitive guide for helping parents navigate the often tricky, but immensely rewarding, terrain of raising the next generation.

It was clear to us that this project needed a writer who would seek out and translate the latest science, as well as the opinions and perspectives of leaders in the field of children's health issues. Stacey Colino, M.S. was the perfect choice and needs to be acknowledged for her professional approach as a writer, as well as her thoughtful and practical perspective as a mom of two young sons.

We would also like to thank the following researchers and experts who added invaluable insight: William H. Dietz, M.D., Ph.D., director of the division of nutrition, physical activity and obesity at the Centers for Disease Control and Prevention in Atlanta; Anne M. Fletcher, M.S., R.D., author of *Weight Loss Confidential: How Teens Lose Weight and Keep It Off and What They Wish Parents Knew*; Ann Kearney-Cooke, Ph.D., a psychologist and body image expert in Cincinnati and author of *Change Your Mind, Change Your Body*; Melinda S. Sothern, Ph.D., professor of public health and health promotion at the LSU Health Sciences Center, School of Public Health, in New Orleans, and co-author of *Trim Kids* and *The Handbook of Pediatric Obesity*; Catherine Steiner-Adair, Ed.D., a clinical and consulting psychologist in Chestnut Hill, Massachusetts, director of eating disorders education and prevention at McLean Hospital, Belmont, Massachusetts, and a clinical instructor in psychology at Harvard Medical School; Elizabeth Ward, M.S., R.D., a dietitian in Reading, Massachusetts, and author of *The Complete Idiot's Guide to Feeding Your Baby and Toddler*.

We want to acknowledge the culinary and creative teams that worked on this book. They include food editors Eileen Runyan and Alice Thompson and recipe developer and former food editor of *Parents* magazine Marla Sochet—all of whom worked to create kid-friendly fare that (we hope!) will spur readers back to the table and the tradition of the family dinner. For his boundless energy and superb imagery, thanks to photographer James Baigrie and his team, including food stylist Sandra Cook, prop stylist Bergren Rameson, wardrobe stylist Jasmine Hamed, and producer Rony Gerzberg.

From the team at Weight Watchers Publishing Group (who continue to inspire me with their talent and commitment), acknowledgments go out to Creative Director Ed Melnitsky, Photo Editor Deborah Hardt, and Consulting Designer Shelley Camhi. At John Wiley & Sons, many thanks to the team for helping us put it all together and get it out to consumers everywhere. They include Executive Editor Anne Ficklen, Assistant Editor Charleen Barila, Senior Production Editor Amy Zarkos, Art Director Tai Blanche, Interior Design and Layout by Vertigo Design, and Manufacturing Manager Kevin Watt.

Finally, a special thank-you to all the moms we spoke to before one word of *Eat! Move! Play!* was written. They provided us with a candid look at the challenges they face in today's world as they are, as they told us, "trying to do right" by their kids. I speak for the team when I say we hope this book will help them do just that.

NANCY GAGLIARDI
Vice President, Editorial Director
Weight Watchers Publishing Group

contents

one

New World,
New Challenges,
Classic Rules   9

two

Discovering Your
Parenting Style   27

Eat! Move! Play!

Parents today are bombarded with messages about the epidemic of childhood obesity. It's one more thing piled onto the already challenging job of being a parent. More children are overweight and obese than ever before. Since 1980, the prevalence of obesity has more than doubled in children and adolescents, and children's health is suffering. The numbers are disturbing and can feel overwhelming.

As a pediatrician, I've seen firsthand how obesity can affect a child's health. It's not unusual to diagnose a child with a form of diabetes that was once so uncommon in children that it was known as "adult onset." High blood pressure is more and more widespread among obese teens and may lead to the onset of heart disease at a very young age. Obesity-related diseases can have such a negative effect on children's health that it is critical that parents, caregivers, and communities do their part to ensure children learn the fundamentals of a healthy lifestyle.

Parents may see their child heading toward an unhealthy weight, but they may be confused about how much extra weight is dangerous and how to fight it. Even as parents try to reign in their child's calories, busy lifestyles often compete with wholesome meal preparation. Parents may feel pulled toward the ease of convenience foods, which are often oversized, high in calories, and low in nutrition. Video games and the Internet lure children away from the physical activity that burned calories effortlessly in past generations.

But now parents have a great new tool in *Weight Watcher's Eat! Move! Play!*, which gives them practical, holistic advice and provides real-life steps to help achieve their child's optimum health. Eating nutritious foods is important, but using language that promotes a positive body image is part of the equation too. *Eat! Move! Play!* helps parents understand their individual parenting style and how that style influences what they communicate to their children. It encourages parents to explore how their personal weight struggles may shape the subtle messages they give their children and how to change negative messages into positive ones. It coaches parents on modeling an outlook that helps children love, respect, and feel comfortable with their body. And it reminds parents that members of a healthy home don't obsess about weight or weight loss but rather practice family habits and rituals that promote good health.

I lost 15 pounds with Weight Watchers, and the process changed my life. The Program didn't tell me what to eat, but it did teach me how to think about what I eat. That experience transformed my relationship with food, and the messages I learned became a part of my day-to-day life. In fact, I've never eaten the same way again.

Through my years of medical practice and my personal experience with weight loss, I know that the simple suggestions presented in this book actually work. The strategies offered here can help guide families to a more positive relationship with food and their bodies so that they can stay healthy for a lifetime. Parents need nothing more than a willingness to make small changes that can lead to big rewards.

Lisa Thornton MD
Medical Director Pediatric Rehabilitation
Schwab Rehabilitation Hospital & LaRabida Children's Hospital
University of Chicago Pritzker School of Medicine

It isn't your imagination: Being a parent

today is different from when your parents raised you. Sure, some challenges are ubiquitous, like getting kids to clean up their rooms or helping them figure out how to deal with a playground bully. But new ones keep cropping up, and today's parents often find themselves wondering, "How can I help my child develop down-to-earth values and self-esteem in a culture that believes you can never be too rich or too thin? How can I get my kids to eat healthy foods given the constant lure of high-fat or sugary snack foods? How do I get my kids off the couch when channel surfing or playing video games has become their favorite pastime? And how can I get them to play outside if I don't have time to supervise them—or do it myself?"

Indeed, the world has changed, and while you may be assuming many of the same roles as your mom and dad—teacher, guidance counselor, rule maker, gate-keeper, cheerleader, and disciplinarian—they have become more complex and challenging. That's because, unlike in your parents' day, your family lives in a 24/7 world—a place where options and information are endlessly available and constant-ly flowing. It's a world where you seldom (if ever) turn off, unplug, or get a day off from any of the roles you play in your life (including employee, daughter, caregiver, and best friend). The reality is, downtime—in the form of personal time for just you—is probably in scarce supply in your life.

In this new world lies a decidedly different concept of the roles within the family, including who's minding the kids. For example, in many two-parent families, it's commonplace that both parents work outside the home; in divorced families, shared custody arrangements are common, with kids traveling back and forth between two homes. Given these realities, many young children spend part of their days with a nanny or babysitter or at a day-care center, and as kids get older, their lives become so busy that they are often on the run, turning to fast food and vending machines or spending more time eating at friends' homes. Stir into this modern mix the influences of friends—and everything, from what they choose to eat or wear to how they spend their downtime to how they feel about their bodies, can be influenced by their friends' choices.

New Realities

Given these new challenges, it's no wonder you may shift onto autopilot concerning day-to-day decisions, opting for whatever is easy, convenient, or comfortable. Think about it: Do you give up maybe a little too quickly and mumble "Whatever" when issues come up about what to eat or how much TV is okay to watch?

Further complicating how you handle these matters is the reality of how you feel about the world around you. If you feel you don't have the support you need, if the world doesn't seem like a safe place, or if you live in an area that's characterized by neighborhood sprawl and lack of social connections, then you don't have that built-in social structure and support system that your parents did.

Yet in spite of the changes in today's society, there is a constant: Just like your mom, you want to do the best you can to set your family on a healthy, happy path. You want to be the best, most responsible parent that you can be. In fact, one area where parents say they feel a tremendous level of responsibility involves their children's health, particularly as it relates to their eating and exercise behaviors. In a series of focus groups conducted in 2008 for Weight Watchers, women consistently said they want their kids to be healthy and happy and feel good about themselves—and they worry about damage to their child's self-image from teasing or feeling "different" if their child is overweight or seems to be getting overweight.

These concerns are well founded, considering that we're in the midst of a nationwide obesity epidemic. Today, obesity is an equal-opportunity threat, afflicting boys and girls, kids and adults alike. In children, in particular, obesity is rising at an alarming rate. Based on the measured heights and weights of nationally representative samples of kids in the United States, the prevalence of obesity increased from less than 5 percent in 1963 to 17 percent in 2003. Among certain ethnic groups, the prevalence is even higher: Approximately 24 percent of African-American girls are obese, while 22 percent of Mexican-American boys are. Between 1960 and 2000, the childhood obesity rate more than doubled for preschoolers (children between the ages of 2 and 5) and for adolescents (those between the ages of 12 and 19)—and it more than tripled among children between the ages of 6 and 11, according to the Institute of Medicine. The good news is that this staggering rise apparently leveled off by 2006, according to a recent report from the National Center for Health Statistics at the Centers for Disease Control and Prevention (CDC), but it's not clear if this plateau is permanent or simply a temporary lull.

Your child's health is not something you want to leave to chance. The fact is, a weight problem can emerge at any age or stage of childhood. That's why the sooner you take steps to introduce healthy eating and activity patterns in your family's life, the more likely you are to prevent your child from becoming overweight—or to nip it in the bud quickly. The good news is that it's never too late to start, especially because kids' bodies are still growing, so their height has the opportunity to catch up with their weight if the right lifestyle changes are initiated. Plus, kids are often naturally inclined toward move-ment, so if you give them the opportunity, it may be easier than you think for them to get moving and stay active.

Yet your instincts are right if it seems like we live in a world that makes it hard not to gain weight. Today's health experts say we're living in an "obesigenic environment," one in which a com-bination of excessive calorie intake and decreased physical activ-ity conspires to pack on unwanted pounds. The simple explana-tion is that it's a combination of not getting enough physical activ-ity (and spending too much free time in front of the television, the computer, or personal game systems) and developing unhealthy eating patterns (whether that means overeating, consuming too many sugary beverages, or eating the wrong foods—namely, high-calorie, low-nutrient fare).

Here is some positive news: As a parent, provider, and role model, you have a profound influence in all of these areas—for better or worse.

As we all know, there are many reasons why children become overweight. They may be copying what they see their parents or friends doing or may have a family propensity to be overweight (yet, on this point, the experts agree that biology doesn't have to be destiny). The truth is, a complex interaction between genetic and environmental fac-tors affects a child's risk of becoming overweight or obese. And while our genes haven't changed dramatically over the generations, our environment has, and we've come a long way from how our primitive ancestors lived, in terms of the types of foods we consume and our levels of physical activity. Factor into this mix that kids may be swayed by what they are seeing in the media as they are bombarded with commercials for sugary break-fast cereals and high-calorie, fatty snacks and treats with little nutritional value, things they later beg Mom and Dad to buy at the grocery store.

Here is some positive news amidst all this: As a parent, provider, and role model, you have a profound influence in all of these areas—for better or worse. In fact, while there is limited research pointing to what works when it comes to weight manage-ment and children, study after study has concluded that your own eating and activity behaviors, as well as your parenting practices, can have a potent and enduring effect on children's weight as they grow and develop. In fact, when researchers at the University at Albany, State University of New York, examined the family environments of girls from the ages of 5 to 11, they came away with findings that in some ways are obvious: Girls who came from families in which the mothers and fathers ate too much and engaged in too little physical activity had greater increases in body mass index (BMI, a measurement that takes into account a person's weight and height) and body fat by age 11 than those whose parents had healthier diet and exercise habits. As the researchers concluded, "The environment that parents create, by way of their own dietary and physical activity behaviors, may have a lasting negative effect on children's weight trajectories and their emerging obesity risk behaviors, such as their dietary patterns."

These findings affect more than aesthetics. The potential fallout of childhood obesity has so many repercussions. Consider the following:

☆ A recent report from the University of Michigan's C. S. Mott Children's Hospital National Poll on Children's Health found that parents of overweight and obese children between the ages of 6 and 13 are much more likely than parents of kids who are at a healthy weight to call bullying a top issue for their kids.

☆ Being overweight can lead to bone or joint abnormalities—such as hip problems or bowing of the legs—in children, and it can make them intolerant of exercise, which can perpetuate a weight problem.

☆ Being overweight is causing kids to develop adult-size health problems—including type 2 diabetes, high blood pressure, cholesterol and liver abnormalities, and obstructive sleep apnea—at an early age, conditions that can have lasting consequences for their health and longevity. In fact, in an analysis from the ongoing Bogalusa Heart Study, researchers at the CDC found that among children who are considered obese—meaning their BMI falls at the 95th percentile or above on CDC growth charts for their age group—39 percent had at least two risk factors for heart disease (such as cholesterol abnormalities, high insulin levels, or high blood pressure).

☆ Overweight children are more likely to become overweight adults—unless, of course, they change their habits. Of the children whose BMI was at the 95th percentile or above for their age group in the Bogalusa Heart Study, 65 percent of them grew up to have an adult BMI of 35 or higher, which is obese. In another report from the Bogalusa Heart Study, researchers found that this risk starts very early: Even the BMIs of preschool-age children were moderately linked with adult adiposity (excessive fatness). Specifically, children between the ages of 2 and 5 whose BMI was in the 95th percentile or above for their age group were more than four times as likely to become overly heavy adults as youngsters whose BMI was under the 50th percentile.

So the foundation for lifelong weight problems is often set earlier than you might think. And here's a sobering reality check: "Obesity threatens the health of today's children to such an extent that they may, for the first time in U.S. history, have a shorter lifespan than their parents," according to recent recommendations for the prevention of childhood obesity in *Pediatrics*, the journal of the American Academy of Pediatrics.

Creating a Healthy Legacy

Naturally, most parents feel passionate about the subject of weight management for the whole family because they understand that establishing healthy habits and behaviors today will help create a healthier tomorrow. After all, most parents want what's best for their children—a happy, fulfilling life; a healthy sense of self-esteem; vibrant health; safety and security; and so on. But in recent decades, figuring out how to help children get those elements has seemed increasingly difficult.

It doesn't have to be. The truth is, developing smart health habits that everyone can live with really is a family affair, one that resides under your guidance and example.

In order to provide parents with trusted information and advice on these crucial children's wellness issues, the experts at Weight Watchers, the world's leading provider of weight-management services, decided to explore the research findings, as well as listen to parents with toddlers and school-age children express what they felt were their top concerns. In the spring of 2008, Weight Watchers conducted an online survey of nearly 450 current and past members, all of whom have children under the age of 18 living in their homes, to find out what mothers, in particular, are most concerned about regarding their children's health and weight. Here are some of the findings:

☆ In general, their children's happiness is the number one concern of mothers, followed by their eating habits and their ability to make and keep friends.

☆ Mothers who were overweight when they were children are significantly more worried about their school-age child's eating habits than mothers who weren't overweight as kids.

☆ While few parents consider their toddler or preschooler to be overweight, this perspective changes considerably as the child gets older; by the time their children reach school age, 25 percent of mothers consider their children somewhat or very overweight, a figure that jumps to 32 percent by the tween years.

☆ When it comes to physical activity, 44 percent of these women engage in physical activity with their kids once a week or less.

☆ Use of television or computers during a child's free time grows significantly as the child gets older; more than one-third of preteens spend most or all of their free time in front of one of these screens.

☆ Many of these women feel powerless to change their children's eating habits, yet the majority of these mothers are monitoring their children's food and beverage consumption more closely than their own parents monitored theirs.

There's no question that the intersection of parenting and food-related issues is filled with challenges. After all, the way you feed your children is an expression of love, a way to nurture and care for your children, a means of sharing pleasure and enjoyment. Simply put, if you handle your own eating habits with a healthy attitude and wholesome choices, you can help your child follow your example.

That's why adopting a happy, healthy medium when it comes to food and physical activity early in a child's life is crucial for you and your children. Yet while many mothers feel an intense desire to do right by their children when it comes to feeding and nurturing them, they often don't trust their instincts and frequently second-guess their own judgment on these matters. As the Weight Watchers focus groups found, while women generally want their kids to be happy and healthy, they struggle with how to achieve that and often question whether they are doing the right thing. Many women tend to be overwhelmed by their responsibilities and are in a perennial time crunch that leaves them feeling like they are winging it when it comes to cultivating a healthy lifestyle for their families. Naturally, these feelings can trigger pangs of guilt, panic, hypocrisy, or angst in parents and leave kids feeling confused about which messages to follow.

Yet you can reclaim control when it comes to how you instill healthy eating and movement habits in your children and a solid sense of positive body esteem. You don't have to let the hands of fate determine your children's weight; on the contrary, you wield an enormous amount of influence in this respect. The key to having a positive influence in these areas is to alter certain aspects of your lifestyle so that you help everyone in the family consume plenty of nutrient-rich foods, reduce unnecessary calorie intake, and boost calorie burning through physical activity.

These changes won't happen overnight. They require planning, forethought, and a mindful approach in terms of how you're managing your family's routines. But they will become easier over time since children are so adaptable and such fast learners, and these shifts will soon become the new normal for your family—especially if Mom and Dad serve as role models. Ultimately, you want to create an environment in which healthful choices are readily available and lots of movement comes naturally to every member of the family.

The goal of *Eat! Move! Play!* is to set the stage for how you can create a healthier, more vibrant life for your family. In order to help rethink and shift how families are conducting their lives, Weight Watchers decided to examine science-based weight-management information and explore the real-life concerns and challenges people like you deal with in the day-to-day business of raising your children. By superimposing these approaches, we hope to help you make healthy, consistent changes to your family's lifestyle in a realistic, achievable way.

Throughout the book, a variety of tools and devices will help you become more conscious of your words and actions, so that you can be sure the messages you send your kids will lead to healthier behaviors on a number of levels. Ultimately, the goal is to help you become a more effective parent, particularly in terms of how you fulfill your parenting roles—as a provider, enforcer, protector, and role model—and provide more effective lessons that will help your children learn to nurture and care for their own bodies in a healthful way. *Eat! Move! Play!* is designed to help all members of the family develop a positive, appreciative relationship with their own body, a taste for wholesome, nutritious foods, adaptive eating habits, and a love of physical movement. Adopting these four essential elements and making them a consistent part of your lives is sure to help children of any age, as well as adults who embrace them wholeheartedly, feel vibrant, strong, and secure in their own skin—now and for the rest of their lives. In this respect, feeling really is believing.

one

New World,
New Challenges,
Classic Rules

You might assume that you'd know if your child was overweight, right? Well, looks, as we all know, can be deceiving, and the truth is, many women with an overweight child don't view their son's or daughter's weight realistically. In a study involving 5,500 children ages 2 to 11, researchers at the Centers for Disease Control and Prevention (CDC) found that 32 percent of mothers with an overweight child deemed their child to be "about the right weight." Meanwhile, research at the University of Queensland in Australia found that 40 percent of mothers of overweight children misclassified their children as being normal weight or even underweight.

In this section, we'll review many of the facts and data that have emerged in recent years regarding children's weight issues and how they affect you, your child, and the very idea of achieving a healthy weight. But first, we'll cover what Weight Watchers considers to be the five basics every family must develop for leading a healthier lifestyle: the Weight Watchers Five Simple Rules for creating a healthy-weight home. We'll also look at:

☆ The latest definitions of weight status in children

☆ The best way to find out if your child is putting on excess weight

☆ The importance for your child's health of consuming some dietary fat and having some body fat

☆ How to effectively address a child's budding weight problem with your pediatrician

The Five Simple Rules

While the idea of maintaining a healthy weight often seems complicated, it really isn't. In essence, weight management is about balancing the calorie equation. When it comes to food calories, the goal is to focus on eating a lot of low-calorie, high-nutrient foods while reducing the number of high-calorie, low-nutrient foods. The calories out (or activity) side of the equation also has two factors: being physically active and reducing sedentary time. These calorie cues are the foundation for the first four of the Weight Watchers Five Simple Rules; the fifth rule holds the key to the power that families have in creating a healthy-weight home.

#1 FOCUS ON WHOLESOME, NUTRITIOUS FOODS

A healthy-weight diet is one that emphasizes wholesome, nutritious foods. Most of these foods are high in vitamins, minerals, and other important nutrients and low in calories. These foods must become the mainstay of a family's diet, including meals and snacks. Focusing on wholesome, nutritious foods not only enhances the achievement of a healthy weight but also promotes overall health and well-being. Some basic pointers around this include:

Choose whole grains whenever possible. Foods made with whole grains, such as whole wheat or oats, contain the nutritional benefits of all parts of the grain kernel. Whole-grain foods—100 percent whole-wheat bread, brown rice, whole-wheat pasta, and whole-grain cereal—also contribute fiber, a nutrient that helps keep the intestines healthy and boosts feelings of fullness. A diet rich in dietary fiber is recommended for children and adults. Indeed, a higher-fiber diet can reduce problems with constipation, a common ailment in kids.

Make water, other noncaloric beverages, and low-fat or nonfat milk the household drinks of choice. Drinking calorie-containing soft drinks is an everyday part of many kids' lives. Between 1977 and 1994, soft drink consumption increased 41 percent in the United States. At the same time, milk intake dropped—a trend that has been frequently linked with weight gain. Experts find that total calories go up as the amount of soft drinks consumed goes up and that reversing soft drink consumption tends to make a difference. One study in the United Kingdom found that those children who simply cut back on soft drinks lost weight over the course of a year, while the children who did not cut back gained weight. Fruit juices, while having nutritional value, also pack on a lot

of calories if they are used as a means to quench thirst. For this reason, the American Academy of Pediatrics (AAP) recommends that the total intake of calorie-containing beverages other than milk, including 100 percent fruit juice, be limited to ½ cup per day.

Include plenty of fruits and vegetables each day. Fruits and vegetables supply nutrients and other healthful compounds that no other foods can supply. They also have a high content of both water and fiber, contributing to a feeling of fullness without supplying a lot of calories. Filling up on vegetables is an especially useful strategy to help children eat fewer calories. In one study of children ages 9 to 14, boys who ate the most vegetables had the biggest drop in BMI. Experts recommend that everyone strive to eat at least five servings of fruits and vegetables a day, with an appropriate portion size based on the age of the person. As a rule of thumb, an appropriate serving size is 1 tablespoon of fruit or vegetable for each year of a toddler's or preschooler's age. Over time, serving sizes will increase. To learn more about the recommended serving sizes for various age groups, log onto the My Pyramid Web site (www.mypyramid.gov).

Take in small amounts of healthy oils. While eating less fat is an effective way to eat fewer calories, it also can reduce the intake of vitamin E, an essential nutrient that is found in certain oils. Including small amounts of oils such as canola oil or olive oil helps everyone, children and adults alike, to get the vitamin E that they need. Using small amounts of salad dressing and sautéing meats and vegetables in canola or olive oil are two easy strategies for adding these oils to the diet.

Be on the lookout for hidden fats and sugars in purchased and prepared foods. Most packaged and prepared foods include fats or sugars that increase calories without increasing nutrition. In most cases, you can find out how much total and saturated fat and how much sugar a packaged food contains by reading the nutrition label, but it also helps to look at the ingredient list: If a fat or sugar is mentioned among the top three ingredients, you can be sure it's a high-fat or high-sugar item. (Keep in mind, too, that sugar goes by many other names—including molasses, evaporated cane juice, fruit juice concentrate, corn sweetener, honey, dextrose, fructose, sucrose, maltose, corn syrup, and malt syrup—on ingredient labels.) Many of us have come to rely on these packaged or prepared foods because they taste good and are convenient. However, preparing simple, wholesome meals from basic foods such as lean meats, fresh produce, and whole grains can take very little time and be just as tasty. Look for quick

and simple ways to prepare meals, including baking, grilling, sautéing, poaching, and steaming.

Always eat breakfast. Breakfast is the ideal time to get a start on the day by eating a whole-grain bread or cereal, fresh fruit, and calcium-rich milk. Eating a wholesome breakfast also offers healthy-weight benefits, and eating the meal together as a family, if possible, fosters togetherness. Research finds that children who eat breakfast tend to be less overweight than children who don't. Making breakfast a regular part of the day is a good health habit that children will carry to adulthood. This is a big plus, because eating breakfast is also linked with maintenance of weight loss in adults.

Strive for regular meal and snack times whenever possible. Eating breakfast and having family dinners both offer numerous weight-related benefits. In contrast, children who snack frequently are likely to eat too many treats.

Have family meals as often as possible. Children who eat dinner at home with their family have a more nutritious diet than those who don't. What's more, children who eat meals at home tend to eat more fruits, vegetables, and high-fiber foods, and drink fewer soft drinks and eat less fried food.

Since treats have become an important part of kids' eating habits, include one or two daily treats, in reasonable portions.

#2 INCLUDE TREATS

Treats are foods that generally pack a lot of calories, are low in nutritional value, and rate highly when it comes to providing feelings of pleasure. Examples of treats include soft drinks, most desserts, candy, and highly processed packaged foods. It's important to distinguish a treat from a snack. Children need snacks because their stomachs are too small to hold enough food to carry them from one meal to the next. A snack is a mini-meal that includes wholesome, nutritious foods.

Since treats have become an important part of kids' eating habits, including one or two daily treats, in reasonable portions, is suggested. A treat adds enjoyment to eating, reduces feelings of deprivation, and supports a realistic, sustainable eating pattern. Yet focus on the phrase *reasonable portions* in the previous sentence: The fact is, as our weight has increased over the past thirty years, so have the portion sizes of the foods we eat. The food portions typically served in restaurants, fast-food chains, and other places are up to eight times bigger than recommended. This is a particular concern for parents: Because our children have never lived in a world of smaller portions, they are completely unaware of what a recommended portion size is. To them, a 20-ounce bottle of a soft drink and a king-size candy bar are normal. Several studies find that kids tend to eat more when they are served larger portions.

Treats can and should be a routine part of daily life. It is never a good idea to use treats as a reward or to take them away as a punishment. Research shows that rewarding or punishing with treats makes them more desirable to kids. Living in a healthy-weight home teaches children that treats are a special but regular part of eating.

The exact definition of what constitutes a treat is an individual decision. Food likes and dislikes are personal and are shaped by age, personality, mood, genetics, and other factors. For this reason, decisions about what to eat as a treat should be left to each family member. For example, while you might choose to have a glass of wine with dinner, your preschooler may prefer Fruit Roll-Ups or a cookie.

#3 AIM TO LIMIT SCREEN TIME (EXCLUDING HOMEWORK) TO TWO HOURS OR LESS PER DAY

Today, it is estimated that more than 25 percent of school-age children watch at least four hours of television daily, and the daily number of hours in front of the television has been repeatedly linked to weight gain. In addition, research is sending an early warning signal that the childhood television-watching habits of the latest generation are having weight-related consequences as those kids become young adults. One study finds that adults who watched the most television as children weighed more and were less fit than those adults who watched less television as children.

The AAP recommends limiting screen time for children older than 2 years of age to a maximum of two hours per day as a strategy to prevent overweight in children. (The AAP also recommends no screen time for children under the age of 2.) In today's media-centric world, this rule may seem unrealistic, unattainable, and unreasonable. As a first step, families can evaluate how much time each member spends in front of screens. Small goals to reduce that time, with specific plans to use the time for another activity, can help. If possible, it also helps to keep television, video games, and computers out of bedrooms. A key benefit of limiting screen time is that doing so frees up time for spontaneous exercise and family-centered activities.

How can I let my children have new experiences in a world where I feel I can't take my eyes off them?

There's no getting around the fact that the world has changed since you were a kid, and opportunities for unstructured active play with other kids or just exploring new territory together are in short supply. While it's important to take steps to protect your children and make sure they are safe, you don't want to become a helicopter parent who hovers and micromanages a child's every move. In the end, this kind of overprotective behavior fosters dependence, not personal growth.

The key is to provide your children with safe, healthy opportunities for exploration and learning by choosing settings that you trust and feel comfortable with—whether that means letting them play at a close friend's or relative's house, joining an after-school activity, or going to a special gym for kids. Even if you stick around to keep an eye on them, hang back and let them navigate their way through the situation. Among the best ways for kids to learn and grow, socially and emotionally, is for them to get out of their comfort zones, master new challenges, and even learn from their mistakes. So there may be times when your well-intentioned desire to protect them could end up holding them back.

15

#4 TRY TO BE ACTIVE ONE HOUR OR MORE PER DAY

The 2005 Dietary Guidelines for Americans recommend that children get an hour of physical activity daily. That is the same amount recommended for adults who want to maintain a weight loss. Most kids currently get about thirty minutes of activity a day, or about half of what they should. Experts agree that the current level of activity is not enough to prevent excess weight gain or lead to weight loss in children. While an hour a day may sound like a lot, it helps to understand that the recommendation includes all kinds of activity, both structured and unstructured—that means everything from playing outside after school to riding a bike to the store.

Unfortunately, you cannot rely on your children's school to make sure they are getting the activity they need. Many schools have cut back on recess and physical education classes so that more time can be spent on academic subjects. Government reports show that in the 1990s, participation in gym classes dropped because physical education was no longer required in many schools. As a child ages, the amount of time spent in active play is likely to go down, and this is particularly true for those with weight issues. Regardless of weight, the opportunities are often limited for older children. Sports teams become more competitive and involve a limited number of athletes as kids progress through the school system. Many schools do not offer options for activity except for their organized sports teams.

Active time can take the place of sedentary time and is a lot of fun for families who play together. A child's wishes about what activities to include should be taken into consideration. While it is a common belief that signing up a child for a team sport is always a good idea, many kids prefer to be active in other ways, and this needs to be respected. What is done to meet the activity recommendation is not nearly as important as whether the child enjoys it. One study found that dancing and walking were particularly effective for increasing activity, decreasing inactivity, and lowering BMI in children.

#5 THE RULES APPLY TO EVERYONE IN THE HOME

A healthy-weight lifestyle isn't just for family members who have (or may have) weight issues. The Five Simple Rules work best if everyone in the family follows them, including those who are at a healthy weight.

In today's world, it is not just family members who care for our kids. If both parents work, meals and snacks are often provided by other people. Left on their own, caregivers may not know how to prepare meals and snacks that focus on wholesome foods. Likewise, caregivers may not understand the importance of getting kids to be active. In creating a healthy-weight home, the rules need to apply to everyone, including caregivers. This can be done by providing specific instructions about meals and snacks, treats, screen time, and exercise. Making sure that the instructions are followed is important, because providing kids with consistent expectations is what makes the rules stick.

The Five Simple Rules work best if everyone in the family follows them, including those who are at a healthy weight.

What Is a Healthy Weight?

Do you feel that you have a realistic perspective concerning your family's weight? If not, you're not alone. In fact, it might have something to do with the fact that some parents view their children through rose-colored glasses, so they may not (or don't want to) see that their kids are carrying excess pounds. But it may be that the perception of what's "normal" has also shifted toward supersized: As body weight in the United States has gradually increased in recent decades, an adult or child who may have been viewed as heavy in the 1970s or 1980s may look quite normal now.

In addition, many parents believe that when young kids are pudgy, it's simply "baby fat," or something he or she will outgrow in time. The reality is, not all kids outgrow baby fat. In fact, researchers from the University of California, San Diego, found that among 1,042 healthy children, those who were overweight during preschool or elementary school were more than five times as likely to be overweight at age 12 as kids who were never considered overweight.

In the past, pediatricians didn't use the word *obese* when classifying a child's weight—but that has changed in recent years. The language that's now being used in the medical community is the same for both adults and children. That means that when it comes to body weight, kids are now considered underweight, healthy weight, overweight, or obese—just as adults are.

But some differences still remain. While the standards for adults are based on body mass index (BMI), which is calculated by plugging a person's body weight and height into a specific formula, the criteria for kids is based on BMI-for-age charts or on gender-specific weight and height charts that delineate peer-related percentiles for growth based on a child's age. Because children have growing bodies, and because weight and height distributions change from year to year, percentiles that are specific for age and gender are used to define the different body weight classifications in kids; this is in contrast to the BMI-specific classifications of underweight (a BMI of under 18.5), normal weight (a BMI between 18.5 and 24.9), overweight (a BMI between 25 and 29.9), and obese (a BMI of 30 or greater) for adults.

If there's any question in your mind about whether your child is flirting with a weight problem, you can find out for yourself by plotting your child's weight on the CDC growth chart, which will tell you where your child falls in relation to his or her peers. Simply mark where your child's current weight lies on the appropriate gender-specific graph, according to his or her current age, and you will see the unvarnished truth about your child's current weight. But it's important to track your child's height, too, to get the full picture of his growth pattern. Your pediatrician or family physician will plot all this information on a growth chart at every annual checkup; it then becomes part of your child's permanent medical file, so the doctor can see how your child's growth is progressing in terms of height and weight from one year to the next. This helps the doctor distinguish between normal, healthy weight gain and excessive weight gain.

Just as the definition of body weight classifications is somewhat different for kids, so, too, is the meaning behind some of them. Interestingly, if your child's weight falls between the 85th and 94th percentiles—the "overweight" bracket—it may not be as much of a cause for concern as it seems at first glance. The excess weight may be due to increasing bone size or increasing muscle mass, not necessarily to excess body fat, according to experts. But in kids who have a BMI in the 95th percentile or higher—what's now classified as "obese"—the excess weight is almost always due to excess body fat. Currently, there's also some discussion about adding another term—"extreme obesity"— to describe kids whose BMI is in the 99th percentile or above, since these children are far more likely to have multiple risk factors for heart disease and other health problems.

As a child ages, the amount of time spent in active play is likely to go down, and this is particularly true for those with weight issues.

The Latest "Classes" for Children

Among children, a BMI that's under the 5th percentile is considered "underweight," and "healthy weight" is defined as having a BMI between the 5th and 84th percentiles for that child's age group. Meanwhile, kids whose weight falls between the 85th and 94th percentiles are considered "overweight," and those in the 95th percentile or above are classified as "obese" for that particular age group. You can calculate your child's BMI on the CDC Web site at **http://apps.nccd.cdc.gov/dnpabmi/**, or you can do the math yourself, using the following formula:

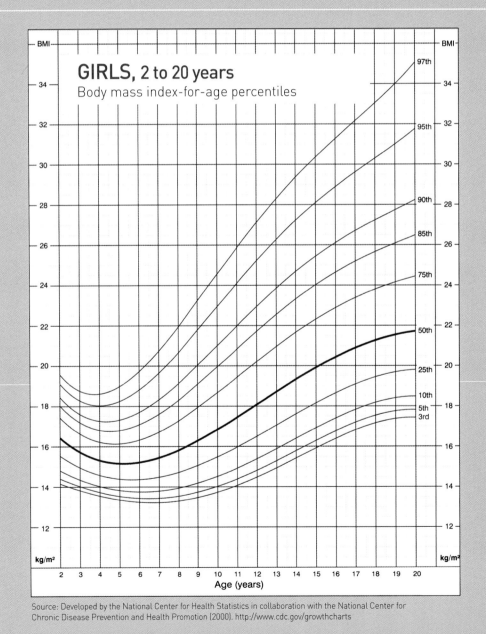

GIRLS, 2 to 20 years
Body mass index-for-age percentiles

Source: Developed by the National Center for Health Statistics in collaboration with the National Center for Chronic Disease Prevention and Health Promotion (2000). http://www.cdc.gov/growthcharts

BMI = weight (in pounds) × 703 divided by [height (in inches) × height (in inches)]

In a recent online survey involving 448 current and past Weight Watchers members with children under age 18 living at home, parents said that their own observations and comments from their pediatricians were how they were most likely to determine if their child is overweight.

If there's any question in your mind about whether your child is flirting with a weight problem, you can find out for yourself by plotting your child's weight on the CDC growth chart, which will tell you where your child falls in relation to his or her peers.

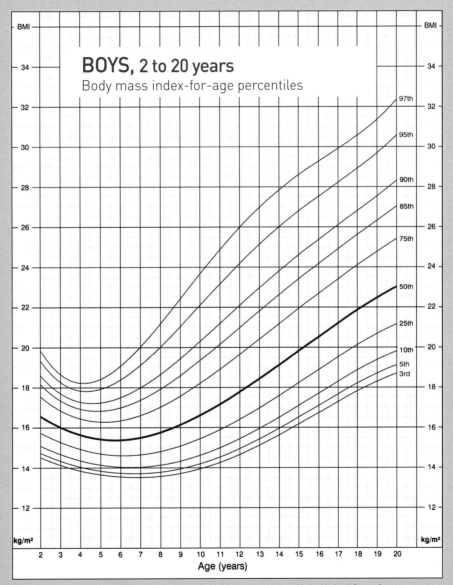

Source: Developed by the National Center for Health Statistics in collaboration with the National Center for Chronic Disease Prevention and Health Promotion (2000). http://www.cdc.gov/growthcharts

You and Your Pediatrician
Speaking the Same Language

If you are concerned about your child's weight, talk to your pediatrician about it. He or she should be able to let you know whether your child's weight is a concern or whether your child is at risk of developing complications from being overweight.

If your child's doctor doesn't discuss her weight with you, be sure to ask. Sometimes pediatricians have so many other subjects on their minds that they may forget to address weight issues specifically, or they may think you already know how your child is faring in the weight department. But by all means, if you're concerned that your child might be developing a weight problem, be sure to broach the subject with your pediatrician.

Keep in mind that how your pediatrician addresses your child's weight—whether she's relaxed or alarmist about it—may be related to her overall manner. If your pediatrician tends to be reassuring, she may soft-pedal her concern that your child is developing a weight problem. If she tends to be a hard-liner when it comes to children's health issues, she may be more assertive about probing a child's overweight status. The pediatrician's style could be similar to or quite different from yours. If the doctor's style doesn't sit well with you, it's important to gently tell him or her so; you might simply explain how your attitude about these issues differs.

Rather than adopting an assertive style with these issues, today's pediatricians are encouraged to ask open, nonconfrontational questions—for example, saying something like, "Your child's BMI is above the 95th percentile. What concerns, if any, do you have about her weight?" If you voice your concerns, your health care provider should then elicit a discussion of what's going on in your home in terms of eating and activity patterns and suggest healthy changes. These might include limiting the consumption of sugar-sweetened beverages and fast food, encouraging the family to eat more fruits and vegetables, limiting television and other screen time, and promoting physical activity each day.

Your child's doctor should also help you develop an appropriate strategy to address your child's weight problem based on her age, the degree to which she's overweight, and her overall health. This can be done by slowing the rate of weight gain, by trying to maintain a child's current weight while her body continues to grow in height, or by encouraging slow, gradual weight loss, depending on the factors previously listed and what the doctor

If you think that your child might be developing a weight problem, be sure to broach the subject with your pediatrician.

The good news is, making changes to your family's eating and activity habits can have a big effect—and a profoundly healthy one—on your child's weight.

feels is appropriate. After all, it's important to balance reaching and maintaining a healthy weight with ensuring that your child's body continues to grow and develop normally.

Take heart in this: If a child is overweight, that doesn't mean it's his destiny, but the longer a child stays overweight, the harder it will be for him to achieve a healthy weight and the greater the chances are that he'll have weight issues as an adult. And the risks begin much earlier than you might think. In fact, researchers at the CDC found that children between the ages of 2 and 5 whose BMI is in the 95th percentile or above are more than four times as likely to become overweight as adults as young kids whose BMI is under the 50th percentile. In addition, being overweight, particularly severely so, also increases a child's risk of developing weight-related complications and diseases that used

How to Talk About It

If there's any possibility that the conversation with your pediatrician about your child's weight may take on a negative tone, be sure your child isn't present. After all, the last thing either you or the pediatrician wants to do is make a child feel ashamed of his or her body. You might save this chat for the end of the visit and ask your child to step out into the waiting room while you discuss one last thing with the doctor; to give the pediatrician a heads-up that this is coming, you can pass her a note about this at the beginning of the visit. Or, if your doctor is willing, you might follow up by phone or e-mail later that day or the following day; this, of course, is the best approach if your child is too young to hang out in the waiting room by herself.

Ask the pediatrician:

- **How is my child's weight?**
- **How is my child's weight developing relative to his or her height?**

If the pediatrician tells you that your child is overweight, follow up with:

- **Is he or she at risk for health complications due to the excess weight?**

- **What's the best way for us to address those extra pounds through lifestyle changes?**

- **What's our goal? Does he or she need to actually lose weight or simply maintain the current weight while continuing to grow in height?**

It's also a good idea to briefly tell the pediatrician if you've had any weight struggles and whether there's a family history of obesity on your side or your spouse's; if there is, be sure to tell the pediatrician about any weight-related health problems those family members had, too. That way, the doctor will have a broader context in which to address a child's budding weight problem.

to be the exclusive domain of adults—type 2 diabetes, high blood pressure, cholesterol abnormalities, sleep apnea, the beginnings of atherosclerosis, and liver abnormalities, to name a few.

The good news is, making changes to your family's eating and activity habits can have a big effect—and a profoundly healthy one—on your child's weight. And if your child develops healthy habits at a young age, he'll be more likely to practice them throughout childhood and into adulthood. In other words, you'll be giving him valuable tools for a lasting legacy of weight control.

Fat: Talking About Body Basics

We live in such a fat-phobic culture. The fat in food is considered dietary enemy number one, and body fat is often not only deemed unattractive but also suggested as a sign of weakness. Both perceptions are wrong—and this is important to point out to your kids. Just as human beings need some fat from their diets for the formation and maintenance of cell membranes, the absorption of fat-soluble vitamins (such as A, D, E, and K), and brain development, a certain amount of body fat is essential for good health. After all, it helps keep you warm in cold weather by providing a layer of insulation. It provides protective cushioning for organs such as the heart and kidneys. It serves as a major source of energy reserves. And for girls, it's important for hormone production and regulation and reproductive purposes, which is why girls' bodies will naturally store extra fat during puberty.

But it is true that too much body fat can be harmful for your health, whether you're a girl or a boy, an adult or a child. Rather than focusing on body fat per se, however, it's better for kids and adults to strive to achieve and maintain a healthy weight for their bodies, based on their height, frame size, age, and other key factors.

Since one of the best things they can do for their growing, changing bodies is to eat a variety of healthy foods and stay physically active, you'll want to show your children how to do this with your own behavior and also explain these points in language they'll understand. You might point out, for example, that if you want your car to run well or be able to go fast when you need it to, you have to take good care of it by filling the tank with high-quality fuel, driving it regularly, and getting the car serviced at suggested intervals. Similarly, your kids can ensure that their bodies have plenty of energy and operate well by fueling them with nutritious foods, moving them regularly, and getting them checked periodically by their doctor (they can think of their annual checkups as preventive maintenance, just like your car gets a tune-up, an oil change, and a comprehensive service evaluation after it has traveled, say, 15,000 miles). You might point out that taking these healthy steps will help your kids be physically and emotionally strong and resilient as they grow and develop throughout childhood.

The last thing either you or the pediatrician wants to do is make a child feel ashamed of his or her body.

Discovering Your Parenting Style

eing a parent is one of the most rewarding and challenging jobs you will ever have. Because it is such an important role, you want to make sure you're confident in the decisions you make. So have you ever considered how you view yourself as a parent or, more specifically, your parenting style? It's almost impossible to answer this question without asking a few more, like: How does where you live affect the choices you make? How does your upbringing—as well as your partner's—affect how you handle your children? Finally, how do your feelings about your body play into the countless decisions you are responsible for when it comes to your child's health and well-being?

You probably have thought about one or more of these questions before. We're suggesting you consider them again so you can learn more about yourself to help you become the type of parent you really want to be. With this in mind, this section will help you:

☆ Define your parenting style so you can be the parent and role model for your child that you want to be

☆ Understand how outside influences—in the world as well as closer to home—affect your decision making

☆ Explore the relationship you have with your body and how it can affect your child

☆ Help you change what you are doing and saying to foster a healthy body image for your child

Style Versus Roles
Identifying How You Parent

Ultimately, your parenting style is a collection of strategies, plus responses to your kids' needs and wants, that you use to raise your children. It's how you guide, teach, manage, and socialize them, and it probably informs how you handle everything from household rules to how you discipline your kids to how you approach food-, exercise-, and health-related matters. If you want to take a more conscious approach to how you deal with your children, you'll want to identify the parenting style that you gravitate toward naturally, the one you're most comfortable with.

By contrast, your parenting *roles* revolve around the different hats you wear as a parent—namely, your roles as a provider, enforcer, protector, and role model for your child. While you may not have given it much thought, these roles are all part of the job description of being a parent, especially when it comes to raising healthy kids:

☆ As a **provider,** you purchase and make the food choices for your family and set regular meal times. You also encourage your children to get out and move when they play, and give your kids other essential tools they need to enhance their health and development.

☆ As an **enforcer,** you set the house rules—including what everyone eats and when, when it's playtime, how much television viewing and other screen time is allowed, when to go to bed, and so on—and you enforce those rules, at least to some degree.

☆ As a **protector,** you look out for the safety and physical and emotional health of your family and take steps to safeguard these elements whenever possible.

☆ As a **role model,** you lead by example, showing your family how to eat healthfully and stay active by doing it yourself.

These roles and your parenting style intersect in many ways. For example, whether you tend to set strict rules or take a go-with-the-flow attitude toward raising your kids will affect how you handle the various parenting roles you play. On the other hand, how willing you are to play each of those parenting roles can influence your parenting style. If you're reluctant to be an enforcer, for example, you might take a more relaxed approach and let your kids watch TV even if you think they've already spent more than enough time

Be Confident!

Becoming a more confident parent sends countless positive messages to your children about who you are and how you feel about yourself. To achieve this, you need to explore your individual style. If you're like most people, you probably use a variety of parenting styles in raising your kids. So to better understand the approaches that come naturally to you, take a step back and ask yourself:

- ☆ **Am I comfortable with the decisions I'm making when it comes my child's eating habits?**

- ☆ **Do I feel as if I'm helping my child adopt the right attitudes and values when it comes to taking good care of his body?**

- ☆ **Do I feel I have a handle on situations as they come up and can confidently take control and guide my child in the right direction?**

in front of the tube, or you might let them munch whenever they feel like it instead of setting limits on their snacking.

If you're still a little unsure of the differences between the roles and styles and how they intersect, think about it this way: Your parenting roles reflect the different jobs and responsibilities you have as a parent; your parenting style reflects the way you approach and handle those roles. By taking the time to explore the differences between the two, you'll become more conscious of how you parent. It's a tall order indeed, but one you're certainly up for given your interest in helping to shape and guide your child's attitudes about developing a healthy weight and body during childhood and adulthood. And it will be worth the effort. You'll take comfort in the knowledge that you're establishing a more conscious, intentional approach to parenting, and your children will have clear, consistent examples and expectations set for them.

What's Your Parenting Style?

There are four primary parenting styles—identified decades ago by developmental psychologists—and each has its benefits and drawbacks. If you can pinpoint what your natural parenting style is, you can then figure out how to maximize the good things you're already doing and refine those aspects that could be better. The easiest way to identify your natural parenting style is to think about everyday situations you might encounter with your children and how you're likely to react to them. Answer the following questions to get a sense of what kind of approach you naturally take to being a parent.

1. **Your kids arrive home from school, cranky and hungry. To help them catch a second wind, you are most likely to:**

   a. Offer them a snack you consider nutritious.

   b. Give them a choice of two healthy options.

   c. Let them grab whatever is most appealing to them.

2. **When it comes to making decisions about bedtimes, activities, and other aspects of your family's lifestyle, you tend to:**

   a. Take charge and believe you should set the rules as long as your children are living under your roof.

   b. Take your kids' personalities, needs, and styles into consideration and set flexible guidelines accordingly.

   c. Let your kids have a strong say in the decisions that affect them directly.

3. **It's a beautiful Sunday afternoon and your child is camped out in front of the TV. To encourage him to go outside, you would probably:**

   a. Turn off the tube and insist he go out and play—or lose a privilege later.

   b. Suggest you go on a bike ride or walk to the park together.

   c. Voice your opinion but ultimately leave the decision to him.

4. **When it comes to your philosophy about being a parent, which of the following statements do you most strongly agree with?**

   a. It's your responsibility to teach your children to follow rules and that there are consequences for not doing so.

   b. It's important to involve children in making decisions that affect them so they can learn to negotiate their way in the world.

   c. It is important to listen to your kids and try to fulfill their wants, needs, and desires to the best of your ability.

5. **You take your kids grocery shopping in the late afternoon, and when you reach the checkout counter, they start begging for candy. You are most likely to:**

   a. Say no and hold your ground. You have a firm rule about no sweets before dinner.

   b. Buy them each a treat on the condition that they'll save it for after dinner.

   c. Get them what they want and let them eat it right away to keep the peace.

6. **When your child breaks a household rule or makes a major error in judgment, what typically happens in your home?**

   a. An appropriate punishment is doled out so that she'll learn her lesson.

   b. You have a talk about why what she did was wrong and what she could do differently next time.

   c. You try not to make too much of it, based on the belief that kids are bound to make mistakes now and then.

7. **If your child had to pick one way to describe you, which of the following would it be?**

a. My boss.

b. My guide.

c. My friend.

8. **You've just overheard your daughter criticizing her body or putting herself down to a friend. What are you likely to do about it?**

a. Interrupt the conversation and tell your daughter she shouldn't speak badly about herself.

b. Ask her later why she feels or talks that way about herself and help her come up with ideas for what she could do to improve the way she sees herself.

c. Let it go, figuring that self-denigration is just a passing phase kids often go through.

9. **You've signed your child up to play softball (or tennis or basketball) and he's feeling quite unsure about the whole thing. To motivate him, you are likely to:**

a. Tell him he's going to try it—no ifs, ands, or buts about it. At the very least, this will be character-building.

b. Take him out and teach him some basic skills before the first session to bolster his comfort and confidence.

c. Leave the decision about whether to participate—or not—to him. You don't believe in forcing kids to do optional things they don't want to do.

10. **While playing in her room, your preschooler created a huge mess, then moved on to another activity in another room. You would most likely:**

a. Insist that she go clean it up, pronto, or there will be no TV for a day (or a similar consequence).

b. Suggest the two of you clean it up together while singing her favorite songs.

c. Let it stay a mess if it doesn't bother either of you or clean it up yourself later.

Now, count up how many times you chose A, B, or C, then read the section(s) below that apply to you most.

MOSTLY A'S: **Your primary parenting style tends to be authoritarian.** This means you probably have high expectations for how your children should behave, with firm, consistent rules and clear consequences for not following those rules. Your household is likely highly structured and orderly, and your children know just what to expect in the way of rules, rewards, and possible punishments. With this style, the decision-making power is clearly in your hands and rules are not open for discussion; you believe that kids should simply accept your beliefs about what's right and wrong, no questions asked. With an authoritarian approach, there's no doubt about who's in charge—you are.

MOSTLY B'S: **Your primary parenting style tends to be authoritative.** With this style, which is sometimes called a "balanced style," you probably set clear limits and expectations for your children but often encourage kids to be somewhat independent and to self-regulate their own behavior. Because you are responsive to your kids' opinions, you are flexible in your approach to parenting and you encourage open discussions, even feedback, about household responsibilities and expectations; this helps your child develop a sense of autonomy and learn to negotiate and navigate her way in the world. There's probably a collaborative, democratic, or team-oriented spirit in your home, since everyone is involved, to some extent, in setting goals, making decisions, and solving problems. But you are able to step forward and exert control when necessary.

MOSTLY C'S: **Your primary parenting style tends to be permissive.** This doesn't mean you're a complete pushover, but it does mean that you tend to be more responsive to your kids' wants and needs than demanding in terms of expectations. Rather than acting as a role model or assuming responsibility for shaping your kids' behavior, you may be making yourself available to them to use you as a resource in whatever way suits them. Parents with a permissive style (sometimes called an indulgent style) are consistently warm, nurturing, empathetic, and accepting toward their children. As a result, you may be fairly lenient or flexible when it comes to your children's behavior, giving them a wide berth to explore the world.

When it comes to instilling healthy habits in kids, a substantial body of research suggests that having an authoritative parenting style may have the most positive effect.

According to the scientific literature on developmental psychology and parenting, there's a fourth parenting style—what's often called an "uninvolved" or "neglectful" parenting style. Parents with this style are not especially responsive or demanding toward their children, and while they do fulfill their kids' basic needs, they tend to be more involved in their own lives than they are in their children's. Given that you are reading this book, it is highly unlikely that you have an uninvolved parenting style, so we won't explore it further here.

So for better or worse, you and your partner's parenting styles can have a profound and long-lasting effect on the health and well-being of your children. Given this reality, it makes sense to take a mindful approach to adopting a parenting style that will benefit your children most.

How can I help my child control her weight without giving her a complex about being "big"?

One of the best things you can do is take the emphasis off size and put it squarely on health instead. Don't even talk to your child about weight per se. Talk to all your children—even those who aren't overweight—about the importance of making healthy choices when it comes to food, physical activity, and other things that will nurture their growing bodies, and guide them by taking those steps with them. By embracing your roles as a protector, provider, enforcer, and role model and steering family members toward healthy eating, movement, and recreational choices, you'll be gently pointing them in the right direction—namely, toward a healthy weight.

Styles That Work

When it comes to instilling healthy habits in kids, a substantial body of research suggests that having an authoritative parenting style may have the most positive effect. In a study involving 872 children in first grade, researchers at the Boston University School of Medicine found that children whose mothers have either a permissive or neglectful parenting style were twice as likely to be overweight as children of authoritative mothers; however, children of authoritarian mothers had the highest risk of being overweight of all four groups.

In addition, a study involving 718 parents of children attending Head Start programs in Texas and Alabama found a strong association between an indulgent (or permissive) feeding style and a higher body mass index (BMI) among preschoolers. Meanwhile, research at Texas A & M University concluded that having an authoritative parenting style may have a protective effect against raising an adolescent who's heavy; in particular, the study found an association between mothers who were highly nurturing and less controlling toward their teenagers and teens having a lower intake of total calories and saturated fat from their diets. And a study from Hong Kong Baptist University found that a father's role modeling can have a significant influence on an overweight child's attraction to physical activity.

Given these findings, an authoritative approach is the one you want to strive for when trying to teach your kids about making healthy choices, right? The answer isn't so simple. The fact is that you need to balance your style with your own personality, as well as that of each of your children. In other words, there isn't a one-size-fits-all approach to anything when it comes to parenting. But since researchers have found this style to be the most effective in many areas of parenting, you may want to give it a try. If you haven't been taking an authoritative approach to situations as they arise, it isn't too late to start. But don't beat yourself up if you can't toe the authoritative line 24/7. The key is to aim to do what's best for your children as far as helping them develop healthy habits goes, while doing what feels reasonably comfortable to you, too. So it may be that you'll end up with a mixed parenting style, a blend of being authoritative on some matters (like eating and exercise) and permissive on others (like letting your kids choose what to wear)—and that's okay. Just be sure to take a clear and conscious approach to matters that really count—namely, helping your kids develop the healthy eating, exercise, and weight-management habits you really want them to have now and for life.

Synchronizing Styles

As you start understanding your parenting style, it's important to realize that you and your partner may have different parenting styles or you may not see eye to eye on which approach to take, depending on the issue. After all, you were raised in separate families, with parents who may have had dramatically different styles themselves. If you and your spouse aren't in sync on these issues, it can set the stage for inconsistent parenting and result in situations where kids are playing one parent against the other. If you tend to have a stricter approach to feeding your kids, for example, and your spouse generally lets them eat whatever they want, you may feel as though your partner is undermining your efforts to help them develop healthy eating habits—which can lead to tension or conflict between the two of you.

It's important for you and your partner to have an open, honest discussion about these issues. Even if you have already sat down and discussed the following, it may be a good time to revisit these crucial questions:

☆ **How do we want to approach raising our children?**

☆ **What did we like and dislike about how our parents raised us?**

☆ **Which style(s) might work best for our children's temperaments?**

By doing this, you'll be able to adopt a more conscious style of communicating with your family. This will help you improve your ability to fulfill the various roles that come with the territory of being a parent. You'll also be able to fine-tune the strategies you choose to use in different domains of your family's life—for example, to adopt an authoritative feeding style (by providing your kids with healthy foods, limiting the treats or less nutritious fare they eat, and modeling healthy eating habits) while taking a more insistent, perhaps even slightly authoritarian approach to homework and disciplinary issues when necessary.

Your Parents, Your Kids, Your Style

Interestingly, the majority of the 448 women who responded to the Weight Watchers online survey believe that their parents and/or their spouse (or partner) have the greatest influence on their parenting style. Meanwhile, 42 percent of the women said they are their own greatest influence—meaning they come up with their own ideas and approaches for how to handle issues with their kids. Thirty-five percent say they are also influenced to some extent by friends with children. Outside influences such as the media, books, television, religious leaders, and pediatricians have little to no influence.

When it comes to choosing and using a parenting style, realize that you may need to mix and match them, or that some may work better with different kids or with different issues within your family. A child who has a rebellious or wild streak may need more structure or authority to help him rein in his behavior and stay on track when it comes to doing his homework, chores, and other responsibilities; meanwhile, a child who is sensitive, shy, or fearful may benefit from gentler support and encouragement.

Revisiting Your History

If you want to raise a healthy family, you need to think about your attitudes when it comes to eating, being active, and managing weight, including your own. Otherwise, you may be sending your kids mixed messages about these topics. If you've struggled with your weight in the past or are currently trying to manage it, the good news is that you're probably more in tune with your actions than most parents are. Translated, that means you probably are paying attention to and being careful about the messages you're giving your children. If you haven't thought about this before, by taking the time to do so now you can ensure that your actions will have a positive trickle-down effect on the attitudes your kids will develop.

Indeed, when it comes to body image (how you see and feel about yourself, physically), researchers have discovered that what matters most is how much a person's family and friends focused on her appearance when she was a child and teenager. Teasing and joking about someone's body can have particularly harmful effects on a person's body image. Research at the Stanford University Medical Center in California found that more than 80 percent of the 455 participating college women with significant concerns about their weight and shape reported getting negative comments about their bodies from a parent or sibling when they were growing up. Moreover, in a study involving 91 pairs of mothers and college-age daughters, researchers at Western Oregon University found that "daughters who felt pressured and criticized by their mothers around eating and body image issues were much more prone to report eating problems and figure dissatisfaction."

To get a sense of how your thoughts and attitudes may be affecting the way you treat your body and handle weight-related issues with your kids, answer the following questions as honestly as possible:

1. **How do you view your own weight these days?**

2. **Are you trying to lose weight or maintain your current weight?**

3. **When you look in the mirror, how do you feel about your body as it is now?**

4. **How concerned are you about your body's appearance, compared to its health and/or ability to move and function optimally? Do these issues have equal importance in your mind or is one or another a greater concern?**

5. **How would you describe your children's weight—just right, overweight, or underweight?**

6. **How do you view your responsibilities in terms of dealing with their weight?**

7. **When you look at your children, do you see your younger self in their bodies?**

8. **If so, does this dredge up mostly good or bad feelings for you?**

9. **How would you describe your relationship with food? Is it healthy or positive, guilt-ridden, troubled, inconsistent, or something else altogether?**

10. **How do you think about physical activities—as something enjoyable, a chore, a means to blow off steam, or another way entirely?**

Without even asking yourself these questions, you may know that you have issues when it come to your own body and body image. Don't shy away from this; becoming more attuned to how you see and feel about your own body, as well as your children's developing physiques, is an important step toward cultivating a healthy—not obsessive—sense of body awareness for the whole family. Knowledge and understanding are the first steps toward shifting your mind-set, making peace with your feelings, and, ultimately, taking a more mindful approach to parenting. For instance, if you know that you feel insecure about how you look or that you tend to be out of control when it comes to planning meals, you can consciously decide to take a more authoritative approach when it comes to fostering body esteem in your kids, feeding your family, and encouraging physical activity. In other words, you don't have to pass down your not-so-healthy habits. By just thinking about how you want to address these issues within your family, you're doing the right thing, and you'll be better prepared to steer the family ship toward better health.

Exploring these issues may feel uncomfortable, but remember your end goal: **You want your kids to feel good about their bodies, as well as to know how to take care of their bodies in a positive, healthy way.** Your thoughts affect your actions, so if you want to improve the way you handle the care and feeding of your kids, take the time to do these exercises. The results will be well worth it.

It's a Two-Way Street

The truth is, the way you feel about your body can affect how you treat it, and vice versa. Among the 448 women who responded to the Weight Watchers online survey, more than half confess to having a "somewhat poor" or "very poor" body image. Yet those who currently have "excellent" or "very good" eating habits are more likely to have a positive body image; on the other hand, those who feel guilty for not exercising regularly tend to have a poorer body image.

Watching Your Words

Children are like sponges that soak up their parents' words, process them internally, then incorporate those messages in their own attitudes and behavior. Which means that how you talk about your own body, as well as your children's, and the subtle messages you send about everything from weight to eating and exercise can have a big impact on them.

While there's nothing you can do to change your own history, you can try to improve your own body image today. And there's plenty you can do to prevent your child from developing a poor body image. For one thing, how you talk about your own body can seep into your child's consciousness, where it can contribute to shaping his or her own body image. So if you're in the habit of griping about the saddlebags on your thighs or insulting the size of your butt, stop. You're unintentionally teaching your kids to cast a similarly faultfinding eye upon their own bodies.

While negative body talk can affect boys and girls alike, it is especially likely to be passed down from mothers to daughters. So if you frequently berate your own body or make negative comments in front of the mirror, you're on notice that your daughter could follow in your footsteps. This happens because daughters tend to identify with their mothers through the far-reaching effects of gender identification. A daughter often internalizes what her mom says about her own body; those labels and feelings then become incorporated as part of the daughter's body image. This is especially true if there's a strong resemblance between mother and daughter.

But Dad isn't off the hook. Research at the Stanford University School of Medicine found that girls whose fathers had high body dissatisfaction were considerably more likely to be preoccupied with having a thin body and to feel social pressure to be thin; this was especially true in families where the parents were highly controlling toward their child's eating habits. The bottom line: Either parent can affect how their children feel about their bodies.

Do as I Say—and as I Do

There's a huge hand-me-down element to most health habits. So if you speak highly of your body, appreciate what it does for you, and treat it with care and respect, there's a good chance your children will follow your example. Of course, the converse is true, too, which is why it's important for you to avoid criticizing or speaking negatively about your own body.

How you talk about your own body can seep into your child's consciousness, where it can contribute to shaping his or her own body image.

Just as it's crucial to be consistent about how you talk to your kids about eating healthfully, staying active, and appreciating their bodies, it's also vital that you avoid sending mixed messages by saying one thing and doing another. For instance:

☆ If you frequently tell your daughter to think about how strong her body is but you often berate the size of your hips while looking in the mirror, that's a mixed message.

☆ If you often tell your kids to go out and play but you rarely do any form of physical activity, that's a mixed message.

☆ If you consistently preach the virtues of eating fruits or vegetables with every meal but a piece of produce rarely crosses your lips, that's a mixed message.

If you want your kids to develop healthy habits, it's essential that you walk the walk and talk the talk—that your words and actions are in sync and support each other. Otherwise, your children won't know whether to follow what you're saying or what you're doing. That's why it's not enough to be a provider (of healthy foods and exercise opportunities), a protector (from negative influences), and an enforcer (of rules for everything from screen time to snacking). It's crucial to be a positive role model, too, by giving your own body the care, feeding, movement, appreciation, and encouragement that it deserves.

Media Madness

Of course, you're not the only influence on your child's body image. We live in a celebrity- and youth-obsessed culture that's on display 24/7, thanks to our media-obsessed world. Thinness and beauty are touted and highly prized, and kids are not impervious to these cultural ideals as they're portrayed on TV and in magazines, movies, and music videos.

If there's any doubt regarding the effect media images can have on impressionable children, consider this: In a study at the University of Leeds in the United Kingdom, researchers had 87 adolescent girls complete assessments of their body image, self-esteem, and mood before dividing the girls into three groups. One group watched three music videos that depicted scantily clad, thin models; another listened to the three songs from the videos; the third learned a list of words. Afterward, the girls' mood and body image were reassessed. What the researchers found is that after watching the mu-

Check Your Body Language

Since the way you talk about your body and your children's bodies can have such a profound, enduring effect on them, it's smart to tune in to the language you typically use. That way you can figure out if you need to change or finesse your body talk.

1 DESCRIBE YOUR BODY. Jot down three to five adjectives that you often use aloud to describe the way you see yourself physically.

1. _____
2. _____
3. _____
4. _____
5. _____

2 DESCRIBE YOUR KIDS' BODIES. Think about some of the comments you make about your kids' growing or changing bodies and jot them down here.

1. _____
2. _____
3. _____
4. _____
5. _____

3 REVIEW YOUR BODY LANGUAGE. Look back at the previous lists—both the one with words you use to describe your own body and the one with comments you make about your kids' bodies—and evaluate whether these words and phrases have essentially positive, negative, or neutral connotations. Then consider this: Are your words likely to encourage your children to love, honor, accept, and protect their bodies? Or is your body talk likely to encourage your kids to become more self-conscious about their changing shapes or highly focused on their bodies' flaws and imperfections? Whether you realize it or not, this is yet another example of how you're serving as a role model, showing your child—for better or worse—how to talk about his or her body. Once you fully appreciate this effect, the next challenge is to home in on how to improve your body language so you can help your kids appreciate their bodies.

sic videos, the girls experienced greater dissatisfaction with their bodies compared to the conditions in which they listened to the songs or learned the words.

These influences kick in earlier than you might think. In a yearlong study involving 97 girls between the ages of 5 and 8, researchers at Flinders University in Adelaide, Australia, found that both peers' desire for thinness and watching TV programs that focused on how women looked affected the girls' level of satisfaction with their own bodies. Complicating matters, a study at Children's Hospital, Boston, found that teenage boys who read men's fashion or health/fitness magazines and teenage girls who aspire to look like women in the media were at increased risk for using potentially unhealthful products to enhance their physique or appearance.

While you can't control how beauty and bodies are depicted on television, in movies, and in magazines, you can limit your child's exposure to some of these influences. How?

☆ Prescreen the TV shows and music videos she watches and decide whether they're appropriate.

☆ Keep an eye on the magazines she reads and seize an opportunity to discuss how and why the glamorous photographs don't present standards that are realistic—and in many cases aren't healthy—for most people.

☆ Talk to boys about some of the dangerous things some professional athletes do—such as taking steroids—to get the super-buff bodies they want.

Think of taking these steps as part of fulfilling your roles as protector and enforcer. By shielding your children from unrealistic standards of thinness, beauty, and/or muscular strength in the outside world, and by enforcing the limits you set on their exposure to these influences, you'll make it easier for your children to discover their own ways of developing body esteem and body confidence. This is crucial because—for better or worse—body image is intricately tied to self-esteem, for children and adults alike.

Modeling Body Love and Appreciation

Besides being a positive role model in terms of how you talk about your own body, you can also help your kids develop healthy ways of talking about and taking care of their bodies. From the time they're young, teach your children that their bodies are special and valuable because of all the different things their bodies do for them: move them from one place to another, allow them to have fun and express themselves, protect them and keep them warm or cool, and provide them with endless sources of pleasure.

If they learn to appreciate their bodies early on, your kids will be more likely to take pride of ownership, as well as take good care of their bodies. It's also wise to emphasize that the better your child takes care of her body, the better it will operate. This will help your child be more invested in making healthy choices for herself.

Here are some other ways to help your kids develop a healthy sense of body esteem.

Make body-bashing a forbidden practice in your family. If you catch your child putting down her appearance or her sibling's, gently point it out to her. Explain that while she may not realize it, saying a hurtful thing about her body is upsetting; tell her to think about how it would be if she were saying this to someone else or if someone else said this to her—unacceptable. Better yet, tell her your home is a safe haven from body criticism or scrutiny in any form. If you catch another adult making a derogatory comment about your child's body—if a grandparent says, "Looks like you've put on a few pounds, haven't you?"—gently rally to your child's defense with a positive comeback about how fast she is on the soccer field, for instance.

Compliment them on their personal qualities. Whenever possible, catch your kids being good and praise them for sharing their toys nicely, for cheering up a sad friend, or for studying so hard for a test. By paying attention to the personal qualities that make them special and by acknowledging their commendable behavior, you will help them feel good about themselves from the inside out, which helps keep body issues in the proper perspective.

Steer the focus to achievements, not looks. What great things did your child's body do for him or her today? The goal isn't to elicit a positive comment about how it looks but to increase awareness about how your child's body had plenty of energy on the soc-

Learning to appreciate their own unique strengths can help your kids see themselves in a more attractive light.

cer field, showed surprising speed during a game of tag, or had enough strength to help carry a heavy crate of lunch boxes to the school cafeteria. If they have trouble wrapping their minds around this concept, you can help them by using examples from your own life. You might tell them how much you appreciated it when they helped you lug in six bags of groceries in the afternoon or when they took the dog on an extra-long walk. Or you could say, "You looked so strong when you were climbing the monkey bars today. How did you feel?"

Praise the healthy choices your kids make. Help your kids take pride in the TLC they give their bodies, which can in turn nurture body esteem. You might point out to your daughter that you were impressed that she asked to go for a walk when she was upset about a canceled play date or that she came home from school and took a nap instead of asking for a snack when she was tired.

Encourage them to look beyond beauty. Have a discussion about who they think is appealing—kids as well as adults—and ask your kids why they find those people attractive. Talking this through can help a child come to realize that a person's attractiveness may have less to do with physical beauty than with being happy, self-assured, or charismatic in another way. Then ask your kids to think about what qualities make them attractive to other people. It could be their bubbly personality, their boundless energy, their infectious giggle, or something else altogether. Learning to appreciate their own unique strengths can help your kids see themselves in a more attractive light.

Offer them lots of opportunities to get physical. Throw a family dance party in your living room and let your kids express themselves through movement. Take them skating, biking, or hiking on the weekends. Let them try their hands at team sports such as basketball, soccer, or volleyball. And give them the chance to try karate, tumbling, or different styles of dance. Besides helping them develop a love of movement and a broad repertoire of physical activities they enjoy, exposing kids to lots of different activities will help them realize just how many different things their bodies can do, which they're bound to feel good about.

Preteens: A Word About the Challenges Ahead

As your kids get older and reach puberty, it's also important to help them understand that their bodies will continue to change throughout childhood and afterward, and that this is a healthy and normal development. But the rate at which they grow taller or gain weight will, of course, vary from one child to the next. Tell them that to some extent, these growth spurts are genetically preprogrammed. Their bodies are hardwired to grow at a certain rate, and this is not something that's under their control. After all, genetic

How can I prevent my daughter from developing the same body hang-ups I have?

The key is to develop a healthy sense of boundaries—to recognize that you and your child are two different people with different bodies and different personalities that should be treated separately. You can't live vicariously through her—nor should you—so let her be herself and develop her own sense of self-esteem her way.

What you can do to help is focus your energy and attention on letting her know how much you love and appreciate her and help her develop confidence in what her body can do, not just how it looks. You might point out how impressed you were by her energy on a family hike or comment upon how far she can throw a football. Besides accentuating the positive observations, it's important to make sure your home is a haven from body- or appearance-related criticism. Don't allow family members to talk about other people's weight or shape, and don't talk about your own body or your children's in a negative or critical way, either.

If you find yourself struggling to strike a positive tone about body issues in your home or you find yourself overreacting to your child's appearance, you may be confusing your own body-image issues with your child's. In that case, it may help you to seek counseling about these matters.

A preteen may struggle to accept her developing body and feel comfortable in her own skin.

factors wield a considerable influence on body size and shape as well as growth patterns. While some children may get a bit thicker before they get taller, others may shoot up in the height department and their weight may take a while to catch up.

Whatever the individual pattern may be, kids' bodies will change considerably between primary school and the end of middle school. Boys and girls will get bigger and taller (adding about 2 inches per year) and put on weight (6 or more pounds per year). If your child is aware that you've had a history of dieting or trying to lose weight, make sure he or she understands that gaining weight is a healthy, normal part of his or her body's development, particularly during puberty. Among adolescents, girls' growth spurts typically begin about two years before boys' do, but by about age 14, many boys catch up with girls in the height department. During adolescence, girls will also get curvier, particularly in the bust, hips, rear, and thighs. This is largely because girls' bodies store an extra layer of body fat to be used in the future for reproductive purposes (namely, to carry and nurture a baby during pregnancy).

Don't be surprised if your budding adolescent becomes somewhat preoccupied by her changing body and starts spending more time checking herself out in the mirror or storefront windows. You probably did the same thing when you were her age. After all, preteens' bodies are going through some major changes as they go through puberty, and as they become more interested in and aware of their appearance, their feelings about their bodies can shift as well. A preteen may struggle to accept her developing body and feel comfortable in her own skin. You might hear your adolescent daughter complain about the padding being deposited on her hips or thighs or your son fretting about the size of his nose or the protrusion of his ears—or anything in between. Body image issues can be especially tricky for a preteen to handle, given the hormonal changes (and the resulting mood swings) she's going through, as well as the fact that finding a way to fit in and feel like she belongs among her peers often becomes paramount during these years. While these struggles are especially noticeable among girls, who may be more vocal about these issues, boys can also have a hard time coming to terms with their changing bodies and their place in the social hierarchy at school. It's important to let your child know that all of this is natural and common—and something that you went through at his or her age.

You might even use your own experience or your husband's as an example of how your body changed during childhood and the teen years before you grew into your adult frame. It can even help to pull out photos of what you looked like at various stages of childhood and adolescence so your kids can see what kinds of changes might lie ahead and appreciate that your body also underwent dramatic alterations as you were growing up. Knowing that such transitions and individual variations in body size and shape are normal can help your child become more accepting and less critical of the changes his or her body is going through. In other words, your reassurances will help your kids feel more comfortable with and within their shifting shapes.

Ten Healthy Messages to Send Kids About Their Bodies

What to Say, What to Role-Model

There can be a fine line between helping kids of any age feel comfortable with their bodies and fostering complacency to the point where they aren't interested in developing healthy habits. Similarly, there's often a delicate balance between promoting a healthy body image and placing undue emphasis on looks and appearance issues. The key is to give kids positive messages about their bodies without overdoing it and to convey these lessons in an age-appropriate fashion; you'll want to use simpler or more complex language depending on your children's ages. You'll want to send these messages with your own behavior, too. Here are ten things to tell your kids to help them accept and embrace their growing bodies.

1. **Think about what your body can do, not just how it looks.** Instead of viewing the human body as an object, encourage your child to think of it as an instrument of strength and power, as a machine that's capable of all kinds of physical feats. Adopting this perspective can help your child develop body confidence and appreciation.

2. **Give it the care it needs and deserves.** It's the only body your child will ever have—encourage him to take good care of it so that he can feel and function at his best. You might point out that this is ultimately his responsibility; no one else can do it for him.

3. **Identify things that make it feel good.** Maybe your daughter loves the way her body feels as it splashes around in the ocean, or perhaps she relishes the flush of exertion she gets while dancing. Encouraging your child to derive satisfaction from her body in ways that have nothing to do with appearance can enhance her sense of body esteem.

4. **Become your body's biggest fan.** Encourage your child to think and speak highly of his body and everything it does for him. Not only will he view it more positively, but he'll also probably make healthier choices for it.

5. **Notice positive changes.** When your child realizes he has more stamina on the soccer field or she has more muscle definition in her arms from swinging on the monkey bars, he or she will gain body confidence and a can-do spirit.

6. **Fuel your body regularly.** Talk about food as fuel for energy and discuss the importance of regularly fueling up with good-quality meals—including breakfast—so that your child will have plenty of energy all day long.

7. **Love yourself inside and out.** Encourage your child to appreciate the qualities that make him special inside and out—his wonderful sense of humor and endearing smile, his kindness toward others, his natural curiosity, and so on. This way, kids can begin to appreciate the bodies and personalities they have.

8. **Pay attention to your body's signals.** Let kids know that they should eat when they're hungry and stop when they've had enough—meaning they feel comfortable and satisfied, not stuffed. By the same token, emphasize the importance of resting when they're tired so they can rejuvenate themselves. Doing this will help them learn to trust what their bodies are telling them and to heed those signals.

9. **Express yourself with your body.** Encourage kids to use their bodies and gestures to express themselves when they're talking, and to choose styles and colors of clothing that express who they really are and make them feel good.

10. **Remember to tell them, "I will always love you and your body."** Explain that you want your child to be as healthy and happy as possible, physically and emotionally, but that you will love him or her in any size. It's another way to express unconditional love, which helps kids feel safe, secure, and comfortable within the family and in life.

Family Rituals and Together Time

As the old saying goes, actions speak louder than words. There's no getting around the fact that it's important to be consistent about the messages you send your kids—verbally and nonverbally—about developing healthy habits. By the same token, you need to be steady and unswerving about how you serve as a role model, provider, enforcer, protector, and advocate for your children. You also need to be consistent in the decisions and choices you make because this will help ingrain healthy habits in your kids.

If you behave the same way, day after day, when it comes to feeding your children, creating opportunities for moving, and appreciating your own body's abilities, your children will grow up believing that these healthy habits are second nature, not something to be questioned or negotiated. This will increase the odds that your child will simply get with your health-promoting program sooner and adopt it for the long haul.

To that end, it's a good idea to think about family dinners, vacations, and the kinds of rituals, routines, and traditions you have in your family. How effectively do your family's rituals and traditions support the messages you're trying to send about leading a healthy lifestyle? How effective are they at bringing everyone together? How well do they create a strong sense of connection and security within your family? And how well do they give you, the parents, opportunities to help your children develop healthy eating and exercise habits and ways of coping with life's curveballs?

Sure, this may sound like a tall order to fill, but don't underestimate the power of family rituals and routines. Research suggests that doing healthy activities as a family has a strong bonding effect between parents and children, as well as between siblings, one that can help kids feel more grounded as they encounter some of the tricky emotional and physical challenges that are bound to crop up during childhood. Case in point: A recent study from the University of Minnesota in Minneapolis found that adolescents who have regular family meals are significantly less likely to engage in cigarette smoking, alcohol use, and other risky behaviors over a five-year period. Meanwhile, in a ten-year longitudinal study of nearly 2,400 girls assessed yearly from the ages of 9 to 19, researchers at Northeastern University in Boston found that frequent family meals protected the girls from developing body dissatisfaction, extreme weight control practices, and substance abuse; the researchers concluded that this was because frequent family meals produced greater family cohesion and greater coping skills (in terms of solving their problems and managing their emotions) among the girls. Which means you're giving your kids so much more than healthy foods during family dinners.

The Family Ritual Report Card

To assess how beneficial your family's current rituals and routines are, read the following statements about common family practices and mark each one with an O for outstanding (meaning it's as effective as you can imagine), an S for satisfactory (meaning it's pretty good but there's room for improvement), or a U for unsatisfactory (meaning it needs a lot of work).

_____ Our family has meals together at least three times per week.

_____ Our mealtimes are generally relaxed, with healthy, tasty food and lively or pleasant conversation.

_____ We have several activities we enjoy doing as a family on the weekends, such as going on bike rides, exploring in the woods, or going to a favorite park.

_____ We each have our favorite birthday rituals, whether it's having a certain kind of cake, going to a special place, or doing a favorite activity (bowling or mini-golf, anyone?).

_____ My kids and I frequently enjoy going on walks, kicking or tossing a ball around, or working together in the garden when we have downtime.

_____ We participate in community recreation programs such as athletic events, charity walks, games, or contests.

_____ We know where all the best playgrounds and parks are near our home because we visit them regularly.

_____ We like to take active vacations as a family.

_____ At dinnertime, everyone pitches in to help with different responsibilities—setting the table, serving the food, pouring the drinks, clearing the table, and cleaning up.

_____ We make an effort to regularly carve out free time where we can just hang out and the kids can talk about whatever is on their minds.

Once you've completed the report card, review the areas where you gave yourself an S or a U and start to think about ways you can improve your performance in those areas. Figure out which routine or ritual is most important for you to upgrade and make that a priority; then tackle others as the previous ones become comfortably incorporated into your family's life. It's worth the effort because creating pleasant rituals that you do together as a family has a powerful bonding effect between family members. They provide a sacred time to connect or reconnect with each other, enjoy that closeness, and share your hopes and dreams, your fears and worries. The benefits you reap from these shared activities will help each of you fill up on love and other positive feelings, rather than just food.

Overcoming Obstacles, Creating Connections

Before trying to introduce healthier routines or feel-good rituals for yourself and your family, it's a good idea to consider what roadblocks or challenges have stood in your way in the past. Consider what has previously stopped you from upgrading your family's health habits:

☆ Is it that you've simply been operating on automatic pilot, doing what comes naturally or easily, instead of thinking things through?

☆ Is it that you don't really know how to make changes that will help you eat right or move more without turning your life upside down?

☆ Is it that you're perpetually rushed or crunched for time and you feel as though there just aren't enough hours in the day to do what you know you should be doing?

☆ Or do you feel so perennially stressed out that you can't even stop to think about these issues?

In the end, the goal is to take a more mindful, intentional approach to creating the kind of family life you really want and to raising your kids in a way that's in line with your core beliefs and values. To do that, you'll want to consider what kinds of rituals and routines will help your whole family feel healthier, more vibrant, and more active—but also make sense for your schedule and lifestyle. If you take small steps to upgrade your family's health habits, you'll probably find that the payoffs are more than worth the effort.

After all, the power of one change is significant on its own. Embrace one health-promoting change for your family (such as going for a walk when your kids are frustrated instead of letting them munch their hearts out)—and the feel-good benefits and the can-do spirit you all glean from your success can have a positive ripple effect, spurring you on to tackle more health-enhancing changes. Meanwhile, you may find yourself making other changes naturally (like snacking on veggies and low-fat dip instead of chips after school). Once you all become more physically active, you may find that it becomes unappealing to overeat or nosh on junk fare because these habits may slow you down or make you feel sluggish; instead, you may find yourselves naturally gravitating toward healthier portion sizes and more fresh produce. Think of it as a side benefit or a hidden perk in making that first healthy change you've committed to. One healthy change begets another, then another, and so on.

How to Make Healthier Choices

No, you don't have to completely revamp or reinvent your family's lifestyle to raise healthy kids. It's really a matter of planning ahead and deliberately choosing how you handle meals, movement, and other matters. Here are a variety of healthy switches that are fairly easy to introduce.

INSTEAD OF: Grabbing fast food or take-out when you're rushed and don't have time to cook dinner

TRY: Picking up a rotisserie chicken and cooking frozen veggies you've been keeping on hand

---

INSTEAD OF: Going to the movies, a puppet show, or another form of passive entertainment every weekend

TRY: Planning a family bike ride or an outing to a park where you can play tag, kick a ball, or find another way to be active

---

INSTEAD OF: Snacking while your family watches TV

TRY: Keeping your hands busy— with coloring, doing a puzzle, or knitting—or letting everyone chew sugarless gum if they feel the need to have something in their mouths

---

INSTEAD OF: Feeding your kids or yourself and your spouse whenever each person gets home from work and after-school activities

TRY: Appointing a family dinner hour and exercising control over when you stop working or playing so that you can have the evening meal together

---

INSTEAD OF: Indulging the munchies when your child is frustrated, upset, or otherwise out of sorts

TRY: Suggesting that you go out and toss a ball or play croquet or badminton to blow off steam

---

INSTEAD OF: Rewarding your child for good behavior or an accomplishment with a sweet treat or another form of food

TRY: Letting him pick a special activity to do together or even a movie to watch together

---

INSTEAD OF: Skipping breakfast because you're in a hurry in the morning or grabbing something on the fly

TRY: Having everyone get up 20 minutes earlier so you can all start the day with a healthy morning meal

---

INSTEAD OF: Having your kids clamor for your attention and something to eat while you scramble to pull dinner together in the early evening

TRY: Reconnecting with a fun activity such as dancing or coloring together, then serve them some veggies and dip or apple slices and ask them to keep you company while you get dinner ready

---

INSTEAD OF: Letting bedtime arrive when it's convenient for everyone or your kids are simply too exhausted to keep going

TRY: Establishing a clear bedtime and introducing a consistent sleepytime routine with a bath, reading a story, or listening to calming music together

---

How can I help my child when kids say mean things about her looks?

First, you can validate what she's going through by acknowledging that words can hurt almost as much as punches do and encouraging her to express her feelings. Then explain that kids are often mean because they don't feel good about themselves (so they want to make other kids feel bad, too) or because someone (perhaps a parent or another child) is saying mean things to them.

In any case, help her find ways to stand up for herself by saying, "That's a really mean thing to say and it hurts my feelings" or "It's not okay to talk that way." If the teasing or bullying persists, talk to an adult who's in charge in the situation where the meanness occurs, whether it's a teacher, counselor, or principal at the school, the coach of a team, or the offending child's parents. Explain that you think it's their job as a responsible adult in that setting to let kids know this kind of behavior is unacceptable and won't be tolerated and to ensure that other kids feel emotionally safe in that environment. If the situation doesn't improve, you can take the matter to the next level (such as the PTA) or you can protect your child by removing her from the hurtful situation and putting her in a better one (by switching her to another sports team, for example).

THE TRUTH IS, you can develop family routines and rituals in ways that are compatible with your parenting style or the one(s) you're trying to develop. Find a calm, convenient time to talk with family members—or at least your spouse—about changing the family rituals you have or introducing new ones. Explain why a particular idea is important to you and why you think it will enhance a feeling of family togetherness, then listen to other people's feelings about what you're proposing and try to negotiate a plan that considers everyone's needs and feelings.

Once you've developed a viable plan, give it a test drive and see how you like it. If it works, stick with it; if it needs fine-tuning, give it the adjustments you think it needs. Above all, try to find healthy rituals and routines that you can incorporate into your family's life consistently. That's the best way to ensure that the habits, messages, positive influences, and loving feelings that you're trying to give your children will take root and thrive.

Wrap Up: Setting Goals

Now that you've discovered how your parenting style and behavior can affect your kids' ability to develop healthy eating and exercise habits and a positive relationship with their bodies, it's time to set some goals. Think about a few specific strategies/actions you'd like to implement in both the short term and the long term to upgrade your family's health habits, keeping an eye on what's manageable and attainable given your busy lives. Taking these steps should help you become a more effective provider, protector, enforcer, and role model when it comes to helping your kids be healthy, happy, and full of energy.

Something to try this week: _____

_____

_____

_____

Something to try this month: _____

_____

_____

_____

Something to try in the near future: _____

_____

_____

_____

three

Feeding Your Family

No matter how smart, organized, or disciplined you are, feeding your family probably ends up being a more complicated event than it should be. That's because it's really about so much more than simply putting food on the table. Feeding your family is often about nurturing, expressing love and affection, reconnecting and sharing experiences, teaching your kids good table manners, fueling your kids' health and development, and instilling positive eating habits that you hope will last a lifetime.

A tall order? Definitely. Impossible to achieve? Absolutely not. Fact is, you wield more control over feeding your family than you may think you do, simply because your influence counts on so many levels—and not just in terms of the foods you serve. Every time you sit down to eat, you're leading (and teaching) your children by example: You're showing them how (and when) you fuel your body with nutritious foods, how you take the time to sit and enjoy your food, and how you eat when you're hungry and stop when you're satisfied. That's why it's important to have meals with your children whenever possible—and to vow, here and now, to try not to fight with your kids about food or let mealtimes become emotionally charged events.

With these goals in mind, this section will help you:

☆ Assess how you're currently feeding your family and help you pinpoint where there's room for improvement

☆ Foster healthy eating habits in your children and avoid common mistakes many well-intentioned parents make

☆ Consider carefully how you stock your kitchen and how you think about meals and snacks

☆ Take a more mindful approach to feeding your family by making smart choices about when and where you dine out or eat just about anywhere else

A Fresh Approach to Mom's Role

Wouldn't it be great if your child developed a lifelong taste for baked apples—instead of the cookies and milk you always wanted—when she's stressed out? Or if he learned early on that every dinner plate should be filled with a colorful array of vegetables as well as whole grains and a modest portion of lean meat?

Without a doubt, you want to do right by your children. You want to teach them about and serve them the healthiest, most nutritious food possible. But this simple statement can create anxiety for many moms. If that's the case with you, relax. Now, step back and get some perspective. If you take the time now to learn what works for building a lifetime of good habits for your family, everyone will reap the healthy pay-offs later. Remember, it's about how you're approaching family meals and the foods you serve your children *overall* that can create positive, lasting habits, as well as feelings such as contentment, security, and warmth, especially if family meals have a relaxed, pleasant atmosphere. Under your guidance, you can serve up meals that may become your children's future comfort foods. You're creating food-centric childhood memories that can leave a lasting imprint on your children's palates and perceptions. So what you serve now really can set the stage for future food choices that can affect your child's health and weight. What's more, if you cultivate a taste for healthier foods together with your child, you'll be reinforcing these positive habits in each other. Not surprisingly, mothers who say their children have "very good" or "excellent" eating habits are significantly more likely to have "very good" or "excellent" eating habits themselves and vice versa, according to the online survey of 448 current and past Weight Watchers members with children under age 18 at home. Knowing that your child is following your healthy example in the food department can give you peace of mind—and peace at the dinner table.

So remember: As a parent, you want to steer your kids toward healthy foods without pushing them too hard in that direction. After all, being too controlling or restrictive about what your kids can or should eat is likely to backfire, and it won't help them develop the ability to understand and control their own eating habits. That's why it's important to make it clear that they're in charge when it comes to how much they eat; you're just the trusted guide who's along for the meal. The key to instilling that sense of responsibility is to give kids (at all ages and stages) positive messages about how, when, and what to eat.

Make Meals a Family Affair

The obvious first place to begin building those healthy eating habits is your family's dinner table. Study after study has found that eating together helps kids cultivate better eating habits and lower their chances of becoming overweight.

For example, research at the University of Minnesota School of Public Health found that teenagers who frequently have meals with their families eat more fruits and vegetables and consume less soda—patterns that persisted five years later. Research also suggests that some children who are overweight tend to eat quickly, so by making the family meal a leisurely affair and encouraging your kids to talk about their day, you'll be slowing down the entire eating process (thus offsetting the overeating that results when kids wolf down food). What's more, having meals together as a family can even help reduce a child's chances of developing risky behaviors—such as substance abuse and sexual activity—during adolescence.

But with many working parents perpetually strapped for time and kids' after-school activities stretching into the evenings, at-home meals often become an afterthought or, worse, a hassle. Kids and adults may be grabbing whatever is convenient for dinner, eating in shifts, ordering takeout, or grazing their way through the evening, instead of sitting down to eat a healthy meal together. With your busy work schedules and your kids' extracurricular activities, it may not be realistic, or even possible, for your family to have dinner together every night. But it is important to try to eat together as often as possible so you can provide healthy meals, model good eating behavior, and reconnect emotionally with your kids.

The Family at the Table

In its latest summary report outlining its recommendations for preventing, assessing, and treating overweight and obesity in children and adolescents, the American Academy of Pediatrics (AAP) stated, "The commitment of parents and other caregivers to helping the child develop healthy habits to prevent obesity is . . . very important. Parents can serve as role models, authority figures, and behavioralists to mold their children's eating and activity habits."

To that end, the AAP recommends that families eat at the table together at least five or six times per week. Sound impossible? Not if you consider all the meals you consume in a week. If you can't always do this at dinner, try to have breakfast together most days of the week. Assess your family's typical daily schedule with an eye toward finding windows of time together, and plan, plan, plan so that you can make it happen.

Food for Thought

If you want to help your kids develop healthy eating habits, it's wise to do a little soul-searching to really tap into hidden attitudes and biases you may have about food and eating. To do that, consider the following questions:

1. Do you think of foods in terms of kids' foods (chicken nuggets, mac and cheese, hot dogs, and the like) and adult foods (vegetable dishes, roasted meats, broiled fish, and so on)?

2. Do you often categorize foods as "good" or "bad," "healthy" or "unhealthy," in the way you think or talk about food?

3. Do you often prepare two meals for dinner—one for the adults and one for the kids?

4. How healthy are the snacks or drinks you typically offer your kids between meals?

5. Would you consume those items yourself?

6. Is food a source of pleasure in your life or simply a form of sustenance?

7. Do you think about or use certain foods (such as sweets) as rewards for yourself or your kids?

8. When you eat a meal, how do you decide you've had enough? Do you eat until you're satisfied, stuffed, or you think you've eaten a reasonable portion?

9. Do you have rules or guidelines—spoken or unspoken—about when and where it's okay to eat between meals (i.e., in the car, at a sporting event or the movies, or while watching TV)?

10. When you're stressed out, upset, tense, or anxious, do you often turn to favorite foods for emotional comfort?

Thinking about these questions will help you get a sense of what you've been thinking, saying, and doing when it comes to feeding yourself and your family. Then you can decide if you're sending your children the messages about food or eating that you really want them to be receiving. You may discover, for example, that you're operating with a double standard when it comes to the foods or drinks you serve the kids versus the adults. Or that you may be making conflicting judgment calls in the way you talk about your own eating habits ("I was bad today") versus the way you talk to your kids about foods ("there's no such thing as a good or bad food"). Or you may find that some of your rules are inconsistent—that you're saying that it's okay to munch right after a meal at the movie theater but not if your kids are watching a movie on TV.

How can I help my child make healthy choices without becoming food-obsessed?

For starters, make healthy choices for yourself and let your children follow your example. Your actions will speak much louder and more persuasively than anything you could possibly say because more often than not children want to do what they see their parents doing. Also, if you stock your home with mostly nutritious fare (such as fresh fruits, vegetables, whole grains, and low-fat dairy products) and you limit packaged snack foods, sweets, and other not-so-healthy choices, you'll naturally be steering your children in the right direction—toward healthier eating habits. The goal isn't to deny them treats, because they'll naturally want what's forbidden. What you want to do instead is let them know that chips, cookies, and so on are fun foods that are to be consumed occasionally; they're not foods that will help your kids grow and become strong and healthy the way fruits, vegetables, whole grains, and the like will.

To raise healthy eaters and help your children develop a healthy weight, you'll want to examine your own eating habits and attitudes before trying to improve your children's. The truth is, when it comes to a parent's eating habits, there's a powerful hand-me-down effect: Whether you intend to or not, you're likely to either pass along your own eating habits to your children or set up your children to rebel against them—a pattern that has been borne out by research. In a study involving 92 children between the ages of 3 and 5 and their parents, researchers at the Boston University School of Medicine found that parents who set few limits on their own eating habits were more likely to have children with excess body fat—not surprising, since the kids may be following Mom's and Dad's example of eating with abandon. But what is eye-opening is that parents who have high levels of dietary restraint—those who are very controlled, even restrained, about their own eating habits—may also foster the development of excess body fat in their kids.

Unconsciously promoting overeating can also happen if you keep an excessively tight rein on what or how much you let your children eat. Researchers at The Pennsylvania State University found that when mothers were highly restrictive (or authoritarian) in the way they fed their 5-year-old daughters, by ages 7 and 9 the girls were more likely to eat even when they weren't hungry but food was available (which is considered a form of overeating). This pattern did not occur with mothers who took a more laissez-faire approach to feeding their daughters.

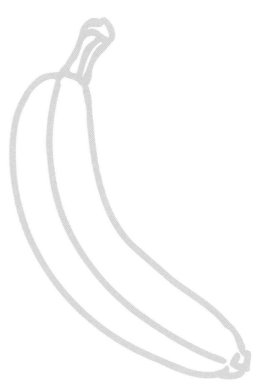

Sometimes Kids Really Do Know Best

To a large extent, young children are innately programmed to know how much food is enough for their bodies' growth and development (though that's not to say they'll always eat the right foods). That natural instinct to eat the right amount can disappear, however, when parents become too controlling toward their children's eating, instead of letting the kids regulate it themselves. More often than not, the parents mean well—they just want to make sure their kids are eating enough or the right foods.

In fact, there are several ways well-intentioned parents can mess with this natural appetite-regulating system, such as offering overly large portions, pushing kids to eat more than they're inclined to, forbidding certain foods, or being too restrictive about what kids can or should eat. These practices are quite common. For example, in a study involving 142 families of kindergarteners, researchers at the University of California, San Francisco, found that 85 percent of parents tried to get their children to eat more during dinner. Moms did this primarily by praising their daughters for eating, while dads did this mostly by pressuring their sons to eat more.

What's more, with very young children, parents sometimes offer continuous snacks in an effort to ward off hunger or prevent or troubleshoot crankiness. But feeling hungry is actually a good thing for kids to experience, not something to be feared or avoided. It's a signal from the body to the brain that it needs nourishment. Letting your child feel hungry occasionally won't harm him, and it will help keep his natural appetite-regulating system functioning smoothly by alerting him that it's time to eat. And allowing your child to decide when he's had enough to eat is also essential for lifelong weight management.

The trouble is, when you encourage your kids to eat (or to eat *more*) even if they're not hungry, you may be overriding their natural hunger and satiety regulating system. This teaches them to eat simply when food is available, to eat past the point of satisfaction, and not to trust their bodies' internal cues of hunger or fullness. This can also happen even if you don't say a word but serve an overly large portion with the expectation that your child will eat it—and research suggests that kids are more likely to try to please their parents in this way, especially as they get older. A case in point: A study at The Pennsylvania State University found that when 3-year-olds were offered a larger-than-normal serving of macaroni and cheese, they ate only until their hunger was satisfied; 5-year-olds, by contrast, chowed down to excess.

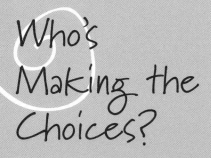

Who's Making the Choices?

In a recent online survey, 448 current and past Weight Watchers members with children under age 18 living at home were asked to 'fess up about how often they let their kids choose what to eat. Some of the things they reported include:

- ⭐ Moms give their children the most power in choosing what to eat for breakfast, special treats, and after-school snacks.

- ⭐ The majority of moms say they monitor what their children eat and drink closely; few are laid-back about what their kids eat.

- ⭐ When it comes to nutritional concerns, these mothers are most worried about whether their children are eating enough vegetables, snacking too much, or eating a broad enough variety of foods.

The good news is that if you feel you have been sending your child signals that may have interfered with his body's own appetite-regulating cues, it's not too late to get them back on track. Kids can learn to become more in touch with their bodies' satiety signals. The key is to serve an appropriate amount of healthy foods, then to let your child decide how much to eat—without your saying a word. It's best to err on the side of serving too little and let your child ask for more if she's still hungry. But if a child is old enough and capable, let her serve herself. To help your child avoid overeating, encourage him or her to slow down at meals, because it takes the brain 15 to 20 minutes to receive and process the message that his or her body has consumed enough food. If your child is old enough to understand this concept, by all means, explain it.

To help younger kids get a better sense of their hunger cues, draw a picture of a gauge for a car's fuel tank, including Empty and Full at either end. Tell your child that after she has eaten, you want the needle to rest somewhere between the middle and the upper limit. The goal is to avoid feeling too stuffed or too hungry; rather, your child should feel just right.

It's important for you to get in the habit of letting your kids tell you how they feel after they've eaten a comfortable amount, rather than telling them how much they *should* eat. If a child says she's full and there's still food left on the plate, so be it; accept her at her word that she has had enough. Helping your child develop trust in his or her own body is one of the best gifts you can give as a parent.

Feeding Your Children Through the Ages

How you approach feeding your children is nearly as important as what you feed them. The following strategies are designed to help your child choose a variety of healthy foods, know instinctually when she is full (or not), and become an adventurous eater. Research suggests that these tactics are actually smart strategies for kids of all ages to use throughout their lives. But remember: The best strategies for helping your kids develop healthy habits start with you and your behavior. So it's up to you, the parent, to do the following:

☆ **Take an authoritative approach to feeding.** This means you decide what foods to offer your family; your child decides how much to eat. Just as you can lead a horse to water but you can't make him drink, you can bring a child to the table but you can't—and shouldn't—make him eat. From a young age, children seek control over their lives, so by taking an authoritative (but not authoritarian) approach—by offering healthy choices and then stepping back—you'll be working with your child's natural desire, not against it. You'll also be helping your children learn to regulate their eating habits to match their hunger and fullness signals.

☆ **Ban the clean-plate club.** Even if you're trying to be thrifty, don't even think about pressuring your child to finish all the food on his plate if he's not inclined to. Pushing your child to eat more than he wants to could result in overeating and could override his natural satiety-regulating system—something you want to preserve and honor at all costs. In a recent study, researchers at Cornell University found that when parents insist that preschoolers "clean their plates" at home, this makes the kids more likely to ask for larger portions away from home; the theory is that because the kids lack control over how much to eat at home, they're exerting it in other settings by asking for more. If you hate to see food go to waste, store your child's leftovers in a container marked with his name or get in the habit of serving less food and letting your child ask for more if he's still hungry.

☆ **Steer clear of comfort eating.** If your child wants to eat at odd times of day or shortly after a meal, you might ask: "Are you really hungry, or are you bored or tired?" Just as adults eat for reasons other than hunger, kids are susceptible to doing so as well. Getting them to tune in to the differences early on can help them nip an emotional eating habit in the bud. If your child is bored, suggest a fun game or activity; if she's tired, encourage her to sit in her room and listen to music or curl up with a good book.

How Much Food Your Kids Really Need

If you're baffled by how much is too much when it comes to feeding your kids, here's help. As a general guideline, serve one tablespoon's worth of each food for each year of your toddler or preschooler's age (three tablespoons of broccoli, three tablespoons of sweet potato, and three tablespoons of cut-up chicken for a 3-year-old, for example). From the school-age years on, appropriate portion sizes will increase, though not in a linear fashion. To learn more about recommended serving sizes for different age groups, check out the U.S. Department of Agriculture's My Pyramid Web site at www.mypyramid .gov or talk to your pediatrician.

☆ **Join the breakfast club.** Your own mother was right: Breakfast is the most important meal of the day. Research suggests that children who skip breakfast are more likely to become overweight, possibly because they become overly hungry and eat too much later. And regularly consuming breakfast is associated with better attention, concentration, memory, and achievement at school, among children. Moreover, research from the University of Western Australia found that regularly consuming a high-quality breakfast is associated with better mental health and behavior among adolescents.

Ideally, a child's morning meal should contain a combination of carbohydrates (preferably whole-grain ones), protein, and fat. Good choices include a scrambled egg with whole-wheat toast and an orange, peanut butter and banana on a whole-grain bagel, or a bowl of whole-grain cereal with milk and berries.

☆ **Serve reasonably sized portions.** There's just no reason to hand your child a plate piled high with spaghetti and meatballs or a foot-long sub. Give your children portions that are appropriate for their size and age or let them serve themselves; then let them ask for more if they're still hungry. Otherwise, by serving too much, you may inadvertently end up encouraging your child to overeat. When researchers at the Baylor College of Medicine in Houston doubled an age-appropriate portion of an entrée, preschoolers consumed 25 percent more of the food during lunch than when they were allowed to serve themselves; this was largely because the kids took larger bites or mouthfuls when there was more food on the plate.

☆ **Keep exposing kids to new foods.** Regularly serve a wide variety of nutritious foods such as fruits, vegetables, and whole grains with different colors, textures, smells, and flavors; cut down on offering less nutritious fare (such as salty snack foods, fried foods, sweets, and the like). The odds are, with repeated exposure, new foods will become more familiar and your kids will be more likely to try them and accept them. In fact, research suggests it often takes between 10 and 14 exposures for a child to develop a taste for a new item.

☆ **Don't fall for kid-friendly fare.** These days, children are (mis)educated consumers, largely because they're bombarded with commercials on TV or ads in magazines for kid-friendly foods (like fruit snacks, breakfast pastries and cereals, smiley-face potatoes, frozen dinners, and so on) that often come in colorful packages bearing images of their favorite cartoon characters. In fact, food and beverage companies spent more than $1.6 billion marketing their products to children and teenagers in 2006, according to a recent report from the Federal Trade Commission. But many of these kid-friendly foods tend to be highly processed and of questionable nutritional value. For example, nine out of ten commercials shown during Saturday morning children's TV programs are for foods that are high in fat, sodium, or added sugars and/or low in nutrients, according to research by the Washington, D.C.–based Center for Science in the Public Interest.

In a study examining the differences in nutritional quality between cereals that are marketed primarily to children and those that are marketed to a general consumer base, researchers at Yale University found that compared to regular cereals, children's cereals were higher in calories, sugar, and sodium and lower in fiber and protein. In fact, 66 percent of children's cereals "failed to meet national nutrition standards, particularly with respect to sugar content," the researchers concluded. Meanwhile, in a 2008 study, researchers in Canada analyzed the nutritional content of 367 products marketed as "fun foods" for kids and found that 89 percent of these products "could be classified as of poor nutritional quality owing to high levels of sugar, fat and/or sodium." Bottom line: You're better off choosing wholesome foods for the whole family than picking foods that are packaged (and marketed) to appeal to your kids.

What's the best way to handle a child who "won't eat anything"?

The first rule: Don't sweat it. Otherwise, your child is likely to pick up on your tension, and before you know it, you'll be engaged in a world-class food fight—about control. The second rule: Keep an eye on your child's growth, not his plate. Picky eating is common among young children, and experts say that as long as a child is healthy, growing normally and has plenty of energy, he is probably getting sufficient nutrients.

Remember, too, that nutrient deficiencies are relatively rare in the United States, because so much of our food supply—especially bread, cereal, pasta, rice, juice, and milk—is fortified with vitamins and/or minerals. Still, if you're truly concerned that your child isn't getting the nutrients he needs, talk to your doctor about whether you should give him a multi-vitamin-mineral supplement.

In the meantime, introduce new foods to your children and ask them to try a bite before they insist they don't like it. Then back off: Don't make a big deal about whether they eat it because this kind of pressure can lead to a power struggle. If they don't like it, let them say, "No, thank you," and accept their preference—for now. But continue to expose them to new tastes and textures, on a revolving basis, to promote acceptance of new foods.

Dealing with Picky Eaters

If you find it a constant challenge to get your kids to try new foods, you're certainly not alone. The truth is, picky eating can take many forms. Some kids may be unwilling to try unfamiliar foods; others will eat the same foods over and over again, day after day, while still others just goof around at the table and don't seem interested in eating at all. Some kids prefer plain foods so they can see exactly what they're eating. And some kids prefer certain colors or textures—like only white foods—and reject anything else.

The good news is most of these picky eating behaviors will go away—or at least improve—with time. Yet until the phase passes, it's important to continue to offer your children new foods because it often takes between 10 and 14 exposures for a child to develop a taste for something that's unfamiliar. There are several ways you can make this process go more smoothly.

☆ At the store, encourage your kids to pick out fruits and veggies they want to try.

☆ In the kitchen, let them help prepare new foods.

☆ Offer this-or-that choices ("Would you like to have broccoli or asparagus for dinner?").

☆ Make new foods fun by naming a new dish after your daughter ("Megan's oven-baked sweet potato fries"), cutting foods into cool shapes with cookie cutters, or serving veggies with tasty low-fat dressings or dips (such as ranch dressing, hummus, or bean dip).

☆ Experiment with different cooking techniques. If your child rejects cooked vegetables, try serving them raw with a dip; if your child doesn't like roasted chicken, try serving it with a barbecue sauce.

☆ Play a food game of taste-testing when your kids have friends over. Cut up a variety of fresh veggies and serve them with an assortment of low-fat dips and dressings; then let the kids be the official taste-testers and weigh in with their opinions on how good (or bad) each tastes.

☆ Vow to be an adventurous eater yourself. It helps if you serve as a good role model by trying new foods and commenting (positively) on the new taste without being overly emphatic. After all, it's tough to convince a child that a food is worth trying if a parent won't go near it.

Once your picky eater begins to accept certain tastes and textures, try linking new foods to the accepted ones and broadening his dietary repertoire that way. If your child likes cooked carrots, try introducing baked sweet potatoes or acorn squash, pointing out the similarities in their colors and textures. If your youngster has developed a fondness for "broccoli trees," you might try introducing their cousins the "cauliflower trees." Once your daughter develops a taste for apple slices, try pear slices. If your son likes black beans, introduce pinto beans, kidney beans, cannellini (white kidney beans), and navy beans. And if your child loves cream of wheat cereal with brown sugar and raisins, try introducing her to oatmeal with the same toppings. The idea is to create linkages between new foods and accepted ones in order to expand a child's horizons.

How can I prepare meals that I can eat, based on my health condition (such as hypertension or diabetes), but that my kids will eat, too?

The good news is that few foods are considered taboo when you have a chronic health condition. You can eat almost anything in moderation, which means you probably don't have to radically alter your diet if you have hypertension or diabetes. But you may need to pay attention to details such as avoiding excess sodium (if you have high blood pressure) or cutting back on simple carbohydrates or controlling the amount of starches you eat (if you have diabetes). In these respects, what's good for you is also good for your children. The typical American diet contains too much salt and too many simple, refined carbohydrates, and these ingredients offer little in the way of health benefits and plenty in the way of drawbacks. So using herbs and spices in place of salt and choosing complex carbohydrates (such as whole-grain cereals, crackers, and breads) instead of the simple stuff will be good for your kids' health. The same is true if you switch from cooking with butter to using olive oil, canola oil, or cooking spray. Plus, by incorporating these substitutions when your kids are young, you'll be promoting good habits for life.

How can I get my child to eat enough when she gives me attitude?

Don't make the kitchen or dining room an arena for power struggles. Remember, it's your responsibility to offer your child healthy foods; it's her responsibility to decide how much of them to eat. Once you understand—and embrace—this clear division of responsibilities, you'll be less likely to get into a battle of wills with your child over food and less likely to get attitude from her about eating it. It also helps to remind yourself that in all likelihood your child will eat when she's hungry. In most cases, if you offer food and then back off without pushing your child to eat, she will accept it when she's hungry, she's low on energy, or she realizes her body really needs it.

☆ **Treat yourselves regularly.** Rather than reserving them for special occasions, treats (which are typically low in nutritional value but pleasing to the palate), such as cookies, candy, ice cream, chips, and fruit snacks, should be a part of daily life—but in moderation. Stick with one or two treats per day and have them in a small portion so as to not let your child munch mindlessly from a bag or a box. The same rules apply for desserts, too. One point on the latter: Don't even think about withholding the ice cream if your child doesn't finish his green beans. This kind of bargaining is counterproductive to what you're trying to teach—and likely to spark a power struggle to boot.

☆ **Set a leisurely pace.** Meals don't have to become a drawn-out affair, but there shouldn't be a rush, either. Encourage everyone at the table to take their time eating and to catch up on what happened throughout everyone else's day. By encouraging kids to eat slowly and chew their food thoroughly, you'll also be helping them figure out the right amount to eat, since it takes a person's brain up to 20 minutes to register that she has had enough to eat.

☆ **Think carefully about drinks.** Many drinks—from juices and lemonades to sodas and sports drinks—are loaded with excess sugar and calories, neither of which your child needs. But it's not unusual for kids to chug juice or soda as if they've been lost in the desert. In fact, children ages 2 to 19 now get up to 15 percent of their total daily calories from drinks that contain sugar, according to a study by researchers at Columbia University's Mailman School of Public Health in New York City. Those calories can quickly add up, and kids don't compensate for the extra calories that are consumed in liquid form by eating less food. Which means kids can easily end up consuming more calories on a daily basis than they need. In fact, research at the University of Ottawa in Ontario, Canada, found that consuming sugar-sweetened beverages between meals more than doubles the odds of a preschool-age child being overweight.

If your child is going to drink something with calories—meaning something other than water—make sure he's getting the biggest bang for his nutritional buck by choosing low-fat or skim milk (whole milk for kids under age 2) or 100 percent fruit juice (in moderation). While fruit juice is a good source of vitamin C and 6 ounces of fruit juice does count as a serving of fruit, it doesn't have the fiber or other nutrients that are present in the whole fruit. The American Academy of Pediatrics recommends limiting kids ages 1 to 6 to between 4 and 6 ounces of pure fruit juice per day; kids between 7 and 18 should have a maximum of 8 to 12 ounces per day.

Keep in mind that on average, these days kids are drinking less milk than the 2005 Dietary Guidelines for Americans suggest (at least 16 ounces daily). The fact is, growing bodies need the calcium and other nutrients in milk to build strong bones and fulfill a variety of other essential bodily functions. So try to get kids to drink more low-fat milk and water and less juice and soda.

Food Challenges at All Ages and Stages

When it comes to feeding your kids in a healthy way, most strategies are universal. But some take on an added importance at certain ages, depending on what's happening with your child developmentally, socially, and emotionally. Here's a look at key strategies to keep in mind during these stages.

Toddlers and preschoolers. While young kids tend to prefer sweet or salty foods—with some preferences having a hereditary predisposition—research suggests that their food preferences often are shaped by repeated exposures and experiences. So don't get into a food rut by offering only foods you know your child will eat. These years are prime time to broaden your child's food world. Also, these are the years when kids often begin to develop their own food-related rituals. So if a child comes to associate certain foods with happy events, he's more likely to gravitate toward those in the future.

School-age kids. It's important to continue to provide wholesome, nutritious meals and to keep introducing new foods to kids between the ages of 5 and 10. A bonus: You can also reason with kids at this stage and explain to them why you want them to try a new food. But you'll also want to bear in mind that kids this age are getting more independent, and their appetites are increasing to keep up with their growing bodies' needs—so they may raid the kitchen and grab whatever is tasty and handy when they're hungry. Don't stop them from doing so; just make sure to stock up on healthy snacks and keep them front and center in the fridge, pantry, and cabinets, to steer them in the direction of smarter choices.

Tweens and teens. During these years, kids are venturing out in the world more without their families, which means they're likely to have more opportunities to make their own food choices and be susceptible to peer pressure. That's why it's essential to instill healthy eating habits in kids from a young age, with the hope that they'll become automatic by this stage of your child's life. You can continue to reinforce those lessons during family meals at home and by praising your tweens or teens for making healthy choices when they're out with friends. Keep encouraging girls, in particular, to have at least two or three servings of dairy foods per day, since these days many girls do not.

But if you start to think your adolescent is getting too heavy, hold your tongue and simply try to steer her eating habits back onto a healthier track, leading by your own healthy example. Research at the University of Minnesota found that when parents nag their chubby teens about losing weight, it just drives them toward the very foods you want them to cut back on; moreover, teens who were pressured to diet were three times more likely to still be carrying excess pounds five years later.

☆ **No TV during meals, please.** Numerous studies suggest that eating while watching TV is a bad idea all around. It's easy to lose touch with what or how much you're eating when your attention is on what's on TV. Watching a show or a movie replaces social interaction, too. And watching more TV can make kids increasingly susceptible to the influential marketing of junk foods. In fact, research at the Centre for Physical Activity and Nutrition Research at Deakin University in Burwood, Australia, found that 5- and 6-year-old children who watched more TV consumed more calories, more sweet snacks and high-calorie drinks, and fewer vegetables on average than kids who watched less TV. In addition, a study at the University of Toronto in Canada found that when boys ate pizza while watching TV, they consumed 228 more calories than those

Ten Healthy Messages to Send Your Kids About Eating

What to Say, What to Role-Model

Here are ten things to remember yourself and to tell your kids to help them develop or maintain healthy eating habits.

1. **Eat when you're hungry and stop when you're satisfied.** It's as simple as that. Your child and no one else is in control of how much he eats at any given meal or snack—and that's the way it should be. Make sure he understands, however, that the goal is to eat enough to relieve hunger but to stop before he feels stuffed.

2. **Distinguish between fuel foods and fun foods.** "Fuel foods" are the ones that provide plenty of high-octane energy and help kids' growing bodies (and brains) develop properly; "fun foods" simply taste good or are fun to eat but are not that valuable, nutritionally speaking. Explain to your kids that both types have a place in a healthy diet; the key is to eat them in the right proportions.

3. **Snacking is not a hobby.** It's a way to keep your energy level high and your hunger in check between meals. It should not become a default activity when kids are bored.

4. **Family meals are a time for togetherness.** They're not a time to watch TV, play electronic games, or text a friend. They're a chance to enjoy healthy foods together and reconnect with each other.

5. **Be flexible about your eating.** Teach your kids that if they overeat at one meal, it's no big deal; they should just tread more lightly during the next. It's really about balancing out or averaging your intake over time so that it stays in the healthy range. This is true for kids and adults alike.

6. **Food is not a reward.** Making it one simply encourages kids to eat for comfort or to associate certain foods (like sweets) with "being good." This, in turn, makes these foods even more appealing—a big mistake in the obesity prevention picture. Reward your child with other treats such as praise, affection, or quality time spent doing something enjoyable with you.

7. **Be adventurous.** Encourage your children to be willing to try new foods and not to judge a food by its looks. (After all, chocolate pudding doesn't look appetizing to everyone but kids tend to love it.) If they haven't tasted something before, how can they be sure they won't like it?

8. **Focus on the food.** In other words, don't eat when you're doing something else. That includes watching TV, doing homework, drawing, coloring, or doing just about anything else. Eating a meal or a snack is an activity in itself, and if your child doesn't focus on it, he may not realize he could end up noshing mindlessly and overeating.

9. **Talk about likes and dislikes.** Encourage your kids to talk about their food preferences and aversions. This knowledge can help you figure out more effective ways to introduce new foods or make disliked foods more palatable—by adding a tasty sauce or dip or slipping the food into a savory soup, for example.

10. **Keep loving food that will love you back.** Once they reach school age, many kids can begin to appreciate the benefits of eating tasty food that's also good for their bodies. So if your 6-year-old starts asking for apple slices with her lunch every day and your 10-year-old enjoys roasted asparagus, go with it and praise them for their choices. It's a win-win situation for everybody.

who ate the same meal without watching TV; the researchers concluded that watching TV while eating promotes eating more food by interfering with and delaying normal satiety signals from the brain.

Limit your child's total screen time (that includes watching TV, using the computer for anything other than homework, and playing electronic games) to a maximum of two hours a day. Also, seriously limit snacking when your kids are watching TV so they won't end up noshing mindlessly.

☆ **Don't give them carte blanche in the kitchen.** Your kids shouldn't have unlimited access to the fridge, the pantry, or the kitchen cupboards 24/7. Nor should they have unlimited eating opportunities at movies, sporting events, in the car, and so on. It's just not healthy. As a parent, you get to decide when and where your kids can eat, so feel free to say no when your kids want to fill up on chips right before dinner (but give them permission to have veggies and dip instead) or to tell them they can have a piece of fruit if they're still hungry after the evening meal. Think of this as part of your responsibilities as gatekeeper and protector.

☆ **Don't use food as a reward.** When kids come to think of food as a reward, they become more motivated by food and they may be more likely to associate food with comfort and praise. This can lead your child to develop an emotional-eating habit, which can result in weight problems. A better bet: If your child comes home with an excellent report card, don't reward her with an ice cream sundae. Rather, take her on a special outing—to the zoo or a favorite park, for example—or let her pick a special activity to do together.

☆ **Praise your children for making healthy choices.** When you're at a restaurant, if your son chooses the sautéed spinach as a side dish with his fish instead of French fries, tell him you're impressed by his choice. If your daughter comes home from school and helps herself to yogurt and fruit for a snack, let her know that she made a great choice. This kind of positive reinforcement can encourage your kids to keep up the good work when it comes to taking good care of their bodies.

How can I make sure my kids have plenty to eat at dinner without feeling like a short-order cook?

Your best bet is to serve one meal for the family (such as roasted chicken with veggies) but to include at least one side dish that you know each child will eat. No-brainer favorites may include baby carrots with dip, corn on the cob, fruit salad, whole-grain noodles, or whole-grain bread. To make new foods more palatable to kids, cut up chicken, fish, or broccoli into bite-size pieces or serve a cheese sauce for dipping veggies. Taking this everyone-eats-the-same-meal approach will allow you to get dinner on the table faster and send the message to your children that your job isn't to continuously cater to their food whims. Besides, this Mom's-a-short-order-cook thinking can perpetuate a child's picky-eating problem because it encourages him to stick with what's familiar and not expand his culinary world.

Four Steps to Healthy Meal Planning

When it comes to feeding your family, it's all about being mindful—that is, thinking about everything from making a grocery list and shopping to storing the food to cooking and serving it. At times you may end up doing what's easy or convenient—such as eating on the run or ordering takeout—instead of planning, preparing, and serving your family a meal in a healthy way. Yet you should know what's needed to create healthy habits and a healthy kitchen, and do your best to maintain both. Here's everything you need to take a thoughtful, intentional approach.

#1 **Establish a regular schedule for eating.** Plan on having three meals each day and one or two snacks, depending on the age of your children. (Preschoolers have pint-size stomachs, so they won't be able to eat enough at any one meal to stay satisfied and energized until the next.) If you can set approximate times for regular meals, that's great, but be flexible so you can adjust to other activities that come up.

#2 **Stick with the nutrition basics.** Feeding your children shouldn't be that different from feeding yourself. For the most part, the same guidelines apply—namely, those from the Food Guide Pyramid, which emphasize whole grains, vegetables, fruits, calcium-rich foods, and lean protein (think meats, poultry, fish, eggs, and beans)—but in smaller portions, depending on your children's ages. Discretionary calories—that is, foods with a lot of added fat or sugars—should be a small part of a diet, approximately 10 percent of a child's daily intake. Your child doesn't have to eat the recommended number of servings from each food group every single day, but it would be good if he or she could come close to hitting those averages on a weekly basis.

To that end, your best bet is to include a variety of whole grains such as whole-wheat breads and pastas, brown rice, and whole-grain cereals. Aim for at least five servings of fruits and vegetables per day and include as many different colors as possible to get a variety of phytochemicals (plant-based substances that have a beneficial effect on your health) in your family's diet. Buy low-fat dairy products such as skim or low-fat milk products and lean meats, poultry, fish, beans, and nuts. And include moderate amounts of healthy oils and fats in the form of canola oil or olive oil, avocado, or nuts.

Once you know the nutrition basics, think about how to conceptualize a healthy plate. Divide a lunch or dinner plate into thirds: One-third should contain lean protein, one-third might have a nonstarchy vegetable, and the last third can contain either a whole-grain food, a starchy veggie (such as sweet potatoes), or fruit (such as fresh strawberries). This approach will provide the right ratio of nutrients for every family member.

#3 **Become a savvy shopper.** Many parents feel like it's impossible to navigate through the grocery store with their kids in tow and leave the store with healthy foods. Not true. The secret is to stick with smart shopping strategies.

☆ Don't go shopping when you or your kids are hungry. Have a meal or a healthy snack first so tempting foods with little nutritional value won't be as appealing as they otherwise might be.

☆ Make a list of the items you need and stick to it as closely as possible. Shopping with a detailed list can help you minimize impulse purchases for foods you don't really want to have in your home.

☆ Spend the most time along the perimeter of the store, where you'll find the major food groups—fruits, vegetables, breads, dairy, meats, poultry, and fish. It's along the internal aisles that you'll find most processed and packaged foods, which generally have less nutritional value.

#4 **Remodel your kitchen.** Stock your fridge, pantry, and cabinets with mostly healthy staples and snacks and limit the junk foods you keep on hand. Remember, you're the gatekeeper, the provider, and the food-policy maker in your home, so it's up to you to take a proactive approach to filling your kitchen with the right stuff.

Limit the treats in your home. While variety is the spice of life, it can also be the downfall of a healthy diet if it's excessive. On the other hand, if you limit the number and types of treats that you bring into your home—by having only one or two types of cookies at a time instead of four, for example—you'll naturally limit the options that are there for everyone in the family. Using the out-of-sight-out-of-mind principle will prevent your child from begging to have a sweet or fatty food that simply isn't available.

Finally, on this point, take a kid's-eye view of your kitchen. This will help you get a sense of the choices that are within your children's line of sight. If cookies and chips

What should I do if my child snacks so much in the afternoon that she ends up picking at her dinner and not eating much?

There's no mystery to what's going on with this situation. Your child is probably eating so much during her snacks that she really and truly is full by the time dinner rolls around. Which means it's wise to cut back on the nibbles. You could offer your child a reasonably sized, healthy snack in the mid- to late afternoon, then adopt a no-snacks-within-an-hour-of-dinner policy. Or you could make a preemptive strike by giving her part of her nutritious dinner—perhaps steamed vegetables with a low-fat dip or a serving of confetti brown rice (with veggies)—as her afternoon snack; that way, you'll know that she's had at least part of a healthy dinner.

are the first things they see when they open a kitchen cabinet, that's what they're likely to want. On the other hand, if there's a bowl of fresh fruit on the kitchen table or small containers of low-fat yogurt or baby carrots plus low-fat ranch dressing within plain sight as soon as they open the fridge, those are the items they'll be most likely to grab when they're hungry.

Get the Kids in the Kitchen

When kids get a hands-on education about nutrition by growing tomatoes, zucchini, cucumbers, and other vegetables in a school, backyard, or community garden, they become personally invested in the plants' ability to grow and thrive. They also become more interested in trying them when they're ready to eat.

If you don't or can't grow your own, take your kids to a local farmers' market or orchard, and talk to them about where different fruits and vegetables come from. Research suggests that kids today often don't have a clue where their food comes from because so much of our world is technology-driven and so much of our food is processed or packaged. By talking to them about the origins of fruits, vegetables, and whole grains, you'll be cultivating their natural curiosity about these healthy foods. You can then take it to the next level by encouraging them to pick out a few new items to try at home.

In the kitchen, kids can also play a participatory role. Giving your child a special "job"—asking your preschooler to tear lettuce leaves or stir a dip for raw vegetables, your school-age child to rinse fresh strawberries or shuck corn on the cob, or your teen to help with chopping vegetables or mixing ingredients—can further increase this sense of connection to the foods they eat.

The truth is, there are plenty of safe ways for kids to help in the kitchen. Young kids can help set the table with utensils and napkins. School-age kids can pour the drinks and bring condiments to the table. And after the meal, everyone can help with clearing the table, storing the leftovers, throwing away the trash, loading the dishwasher, and so on. This way, home-cooked healthy meals will truly become a family affair, and it'll be another positive way for kids to spend quality time with Mom and Dad.

Easy Substitutions That Won't Skimp on Flavor

If you start buying lower-fat versions of your kids' favorite foods and making smart substitutions whenever possible, you can save everyone in the family loads of fat and unnecessary calories each day without sacrificing flavor. Here's how.

INSTEAD OF BUYING:	BUY:
Ground beef for burgers	Ground turkey breast or 95% lean ground beef
Chicken nuggets or tenders	Chicken you can cut into strips and bake or grill
Hot dogs	97% fat-free franks
French fries	Oven-baked fries
Regular cheese or yogurt	Low-fat cheese or yogurt
Regular margarine	Reduced-fat margarine
Regular salad dressing	Low-fat salad dressing
Tortilla chips	Baked tortilla chips
Microwave popcorn, butter	Low-fat microwave popcorn
Ice cream	Low-fat ice cream or frozen yogurt

Dining Out with Kids

Given today's hectic lifestyles, it's hardly surprising that people are eating out at restaurants more often. By some estimates, the average household spends 40 percent of its food money on eating away from home, whether that means dining at a restaurant or getting takeout or fast food. But this habit comes with some weighty (pun intended) risks: Since you don't have control over how the food is prepared, you have no way of knowing how much fat or how many calories it contains. Plus restaurant meals are subject to incredible portion distortion, often offering enough for two or three meals.

Children who eat out frequently score worse on measures of heart disease risk than those who eat more meals at home.

Considering these realities, it's no wonder children who eat out frequently score worse on measures of heart disease risk than those who eat more meals at home, according to researchers at the Cardiovascular Research and Education Foundation in Wausau, Wisconsin. Specifically, the research found that kids in the second, fifth, eighth, and eleventh grades who eat out more than four times per week (not including lunches in the school cafeteria) have significantly higher blood pressure, lower levels of healthy HDL cholesterol, smaller particle size of (harmful) LDL cholesterol, and lower insulin sensitivity than their peers who eat out less often.

Meanwhile, consuming fast food frequently can also increase a child's risk of packing on extra pounds. In a study involving 6,212 kids between the ages of 4 and 19, researchers at the U.S. Department of Agriculture found that on a typical day 30 percent of kids consume fast food. Those who eat fast food consumed more total calories, more total fat, more added sugars, more sugar-sweetened beverages, less fiber, and fewer fruits and nonstarchy vegetables compared to those who do not eat fast food. While there's nothing wrong with occasionally eating fast food, it's best to consider these outings a treat, not a frequent occurrence.

Wherever you go to dine out or get takeout, it's best to take a proactive approach to making eating out with kids a healthy *and* enjoyable experience. Here's how.

☆ Select restaurants that offer healthier children's menus, not just items such as macaroni and cheese or chicken tenders.

☆ Avoid all-you-can-eat buffets, which naturally encourage sampling lots of different dishes and can easily lead to overeating.

☆ Decode the menu and try to avoid anything described as "crispy" or "crusted," since this usually means fried; steer your kids toward baked, grilled, steamed, or broiled items instead.

☆ Ask to have the sauce or dressing served on the side, to minimize the amount of fat your child consumes.

☆ Ask to substitute healthier side dishes such as a fruit cup or veggies for the fries.

☆ Suggest two or three healthy items from the menu, then let your child choose the one he or she wants.

☆ Set aside the excess to take home in a doggie bag so your child can enjoy it the next day.

What's the best way to handle a child's request to buy junk foods he saw on TV or had at a friend's house?

It's okay to occasionally buy a snack food or sweet item that your child is begging for, but do it as a special treat, not as a regular occurrence. And when you do give in, buy these items one at a time instead of stocking up on several at once. Keep in mind, too, that your child's initial enthusiasm for something he saw on TV or had at a friend's house may fade with time or he may forget about it entirely. So if you listen to his request and say that someday he can try them, that may be enough satisfy his desire as much as actually buying and trying them would.

The New Thinking on Lunch

If you've run out of ideas for healthy lunches to pack for your kids, no worries. You want to make sure that your kids look forward to what you've packed so that they won't throw their lunches away uneaten or opt for the cafeteria's high-fat offerings. If you're ready to move beyond the standard PB&J and spice up the lunches they bring to school, try these healthy suggestions:

- ☆ A whole-wheat tortilla roll-up with a slice of lean ham and low-fat cheese or cream cheese, lettuce, and tomato; a small bag of grapes; a small carton of low-fat yogurt

- ☆ Whole-grain pasta salad with cherry tomatoes, peas, shredded carrots, and small chunks of mozzarella cheese; an apple; a small carton of low-fat milk

- ☆ A container of low-fat cottage cheese topped with fruit salad; whole-grain crackers

- ☆ A whole-wheat pita pocket stuffed with hummus, shredded carrots, and lettuce; string cheese; canned peaches (in light syrup or their own juice) or fresh strawberries

- ☆ Chicken salad with low-fat mayo and chopped celery and grapes; a whole-grain roll; a yogurt stick

- ☆ Nothing but finger foods: low-fat cheese and whole-grain crackers; baby carrots and low-fat ranch dip; blueberries and raspberries

Smart Snacks to Pack

Show your child how to eat healthfully when you're out. Pack an apple or a banana for an easy, portable snack, or bring a bag of edamame with you. Keep a couple of whole-grain granola bars—ones that are lower in fat and sugar—or a bag of homemade trail mix (with a low-fat whole-grain cereal, almonds, walnuts, and dried fruits such as raisins, apricots, and cranberries) in your purse or briefcase. And carry a water bottle with you so you won't have to buy juice or soda if you get thirsty when you're out and about.

How should I handle it when other people—such as family members, friends, or neighbors—undermine or sabotage the healthy eating habits I'm trying to instill?

It's important to talk with other people who take care of your children—including day-care workers, nannies, babysitters, and perhaps other family members—about how you would like your children to eat. Make your wishes known, then trust that they'll follow them—or consider switching sitters, for example, if yours doesn't comply with your requests and routinely lets your kids overdose on junk food to the point where they feel sick. But try to remain somewhat flexible: Having a certain type of cookies at a friend's house after school or letting Grandma spoil your kids with extra fun food once in a while won't do any lasting harm to your children. And if you consistently serve your kids healthy foods at home, you'll be counteracting these occasional influences in a positive way. Remember that your goal is to instill healthy eating habits in your kids while also teaching them how to handle treats and occasional splurges in the real world—in moderation.

77

How can I reward my child for making healthy choices without using food as a reward?

For starters, stop thinking about food as even a possible reward and start thinking outside the (ice)box. There's a whole host of rewards you could give your child on a daily, weekly, monthly, or even spontaneous basis for healthy behavior. Verbal praise, hugs and kisses, and quality time with a beloved parent are at the top of many kids' wish lists. So if your child reaches a goal of consuming five servings of fruits and vegetables daily for a week—you might even keep track on a sticker chart, to make it fun— you could reward her with hugs, high fives, and an activity of her choice (a special bike ride, a marathon coloring session together, or something else) that doesn't involve food. Similarly, if your child reaches a new personal best when it comes to doing something physical (such as riding his bike or jumping rope) instead of snacking when he's bored, you might reward him with some new gear that's related to his chosen pursuit (a new bell for his bike or a new jump rope, for example).

Wrap Up: Setting Goals

Now that you've discovered how your approach to feeding your family can have a lasting effect on your kids and what they really need in the way of nutrition and encouragement, it's time to set some goals.

Think about a few specific strategies you'd like to implement in both the short term and the long term to upgrade your family's eating habits, keeping an eye on what's realistic and manageable given your hectic schedules. Taking these steps should help you become a more effective provider, protector, enforcer, and role model when it comes to helping your kids develop healthy eating habits and attitudes about food—now and for life.

Something to try this week: _____

_____

_____

_____

Something to try this month: _____

_____

_____

_____

Something to try in the near future: _____

_____

_____

_____

four

Moving and Playing

*G*et moving! Go out and play! Just do it!

These fitness-focused sound bites are alive and well—but is anyone really listening to them? For too many parents, as well as their kids, an afternoon of sitting in front of their screen of choice is the preferred activity. Think about it: How much physical activity does your family regularly include in their daily life? Given the choice, on a Saturday or Sunday afternoon, are you more likely to go to a movie with your kids or take a bike ride? Do you ever talk about movement with your kids, or is the subject off your radar screen entirely?

Here's a reality check: If you want to raise a healthy family, regular physical activity has to become part of the picture for everyone. You probably realize that encouraging your child to be physically active from an early age will lower his chances of becoming overweight and reduce his risks of developing various weight-related diseases such as heart disease, high blood pressure, type 2 diabetes, and even some forms of cancer. After all, study after study has found a correlation between a lack of physical activity and being overweight among children. Besides burning calories and boosting metabolism around the clock, regular physical activity can also build and preserve muscle mass and reduce how much fat is carried on a child's body.

Indeed, the health benefits of regular physical activity are so powerful for everyone—kids, teens, and adults—that you really can't go wrong by incorporating more movement of any type in your family's life.

With this in mind, this section will help you:

☆ Assess your current attitudes toward physical activity and how much exercise your family is getting on a regular basis

☆ Explore the obstacles that prevent you and your kids from engaging in regular physical activity

☆ Evaluate the movement-related messages you're sending to your kids in terms of what you're thinking, saying, and doing—and how you can improve upon them

☆ Figure out how you can incorporate more movement into your family's everyday life in creative, fun-filled ways

Head-to-Toe Benefits

When it comes to physical activity, actions definitely speak louder than words, and that's why your roles as provider, enforcer, protector, and role model are critical when it comes to movement, too. Yet the reality is that when you become a parent, your to-do list doubles, triples, and sometimes quadruples. There have undoubtedly been countless times when you've felt like something's got to give—and exercise becomes the thing that gives, simply because it doesn't seem like such a priority when you have so many more pressing demands on your time.

But you need to do your best to make exercise a priority. There's no question that regular exercise has a profound effect on weight management and the development of healthy habits, among kids and adults alike. In fact, there's a bit of a seesaw effect at work: As a child's weight rises above the normal threshold, physical fitness typically goes down; conversely, as a child's level of physical fitness goes up, his or her weight is likely to go down into a healthier range.

Yet physical activity also does so much more than simply help with weight control. Consider the following:

☆ **Regular movement enhances a child's overall health as well as his mood and self-image**—so much so that some experts now distinguish between below-the-neck benefits and above-the-neck benefits of exercise for kids. Below-the-neck benefits include building cardiovascular fitness, developing healthy bones and lungs, improving muscle strength and endurance, enhancing immune function, improving blood pressure and cholesterol levels, and helping to control body weight. Above-the-neck benefits include reducing stress, anxiety, and depression and boosting self-esteem and body image. In fact, a study at Old Dominion University in Norfolk, Virginia, found that when girls between the ages of 8 and 12 participated in a curriculum-based running program called Girls on the Run, they experienced a significant improvement in measures of self-esteem, body size satisfaction, and eating attitudes/behavior from the beginning of the program to the end.

☆ **Being physically active can enhance thinking abilities and help kids perform** (and behave) better in school. In a recent study involving more than 1,800 kids in fourth, sixth, seventh, and eighth grade, researchers at Harvard Medical School found that kids who passed numerous fitness tests were more likely to score well on measures of academic achievement in both English and math. In addition, a study

How can I get my kids to try new sports?

The best thing to do is to teach your kids some of the basic skills for a particular sport—basketball or soccer, for example—in your own backyard or at the park or a gym before signing them up for a team. Keep it light and playful; don't make it a macho or competitive experience or you're bound to turn off your kids (and perhaps do a number on their self-esteem in the process). Make the learning process as much fun as possible by playing silly games that involve dribbling, for instance, rather than having them do hard-core drills. When your child does something well, heap on the praise, which will serve as positive reinforcement. If your child isn't getting the hang of it, shift gears and try something else—say, shooting or passing the ball instead of dribbling. Once your child has developed some of the basic skills and is interested in actually playing the game, sign him or her up for a developmentally appropriate team that plays all the players (not just the best ones) and emphasizes having fun over winning. This will boost the chances of it being an enjoyable experience for him or her.

by researchers at the University of Illinois in Urbana found that aerobic capacity—as measured by field tests of physical fitness—among 259 kids in third and fifth grade was positively associated with total academic achievement, math achievement, and reading achievement. So you might just see a difference on their report cards, too!

Finding Real-World Solutions

Yet thanks to technology and real-world habits, many kids spend more time each day parked in front of TV, computer, and electronic-game screens than moving their bodies. Neighborhood sprawl and the loss of a sense of community in many suburbs have made it harder for kids to safely play outside without close parental supervision. Meanwhile, with nationwide cutbacks in physical education (PE) in public schools, you can't count on your child getting enough movement at school, either. In fact, while the National Association for Sport and Physical Education recommends 150 minutes of PE per week for kids in elementary school and 225 minutes per week for those in middle or high school, in many public school districts, kids have PE just once a week now, not every day. And you can't rest assured that they'll make up for that loss of movement at recess; many kids sit around and chat with their friends during this free time.

That's why it's essential to think of physical fitness as a family affair and incorporate it into your family's life in all sorts of ways, big and small. Encouraging your children to be physically active from an early age can help instill a lifelong love of movement that can, in turn, help prevent a variety of risk factors that can lead to chronic diseases later in life.

Your Roles, Your Family, and Exercise

Here's the good news: The exercise habits you role-model for your children and the suggestions you make about how and when they should move their bodies can have a powerful impact on your kids. (And knowing this might be just the push you need to commit to moving your own body more!) Sure, sometimes you may need to be an enforcer, giving kids a verbal push to get moving instead of parking themselves in front of a computer screen. In fact, research has found that your parenting style can make a difference with exercise, too. In a study involving 812 Latino parents and their children in kindergarten through second grade, researchers at San Diego State University found that when parents used positive reinforcement and monitoring, their children were more likely to have healthy eating and exercise habits compared to children of parents who had a highly controlling (authoritarian) style.

Want more incentive (and proof) that you're the role model when it comes to getting your kids to develop a lifelong love for fitness?

☆ In a study involving 8,484 kids from 7 to 15 years old, researchers at the University of Tasmania in Australia found that parental exercise was positively associated with children's extracurricular sports participation and their cardiorespiratory fitness levels.

☆ In a study involving 13,246 adolescents, researchers at the University of North Carolina at Chapel Hill found that family cohesion and parental engagement in physical activity positively predicted teens participating in five or more bouts of moderate-to-vigorous physical activity per week a year later.

☆ In a study with 2,379 girls who were 9 and 10 years old, researchers at the University of California, San Francisco, found that girls whose parents exercised three or more times per week were about 50 percent more active than girls with sedentary parents— and they remained more active over the next nine years.

Yet the responsibility for getting your child to move more needn't solely be Mom's. Consider this: Research at the University of Missouri at Columbia found that while a child's enjoyment (early on) of physical activity was the only consistent predictor of ongoing physical activity in fifth or sixth grade, other factors come into play as time goes on, including a child's knowledge about exercise. Role-modeling and support from friends

To get and keep kids moving, physical activity really does need to start at home.

and parents were important predictors of eighth- and ninth-grade girls' activity levels. By contrast, boys of the same age were heavily influenced by their own self-efficacy (confidence) about their abilities, their exercise knowledge, parental modeling, and their interest in media coverage of sports. As the researchers concluded, "Socialization in the family unit exerts a tremendous influence on health-related behaviors such as exercise."

But the potential payoff goes the other way, too, and can benefit the family as a unit. "Children's involvement with sports is associated with higher levels of family satisfaction," concluded a recent report by the Women's Sports Foundation, which conducted a nation-wide, school-based survey of 2,185 girls and boys in third through twelfth grades. In other words, it may be that a family that plays together actually stays happier together.

So to get and keep kids moving, physical activity really does need to start at home. If you're already in the exercise habit, it's not enough for your kids to just hear *you* talk about going to the gym. For your influence to actually encourage *them* to get physical, they need to see you in action—on a treadmill, on a court, or in a cycling class, for instance. They need you to show them that moving your body is important to you and worth the time and energy you spend doing it. For kids, seeing really is believing: When they see you carve out time from your busy schedule to get physical, they're more likely to follow your example because they'll realize what a priority it is for you—and perhaps should be for them.

Your actions concerning movement are simple, powerful ways to send the right message to your kids. You can role-model healthy movement just by incorporating more of it into your daily habits—like taking the stairs with your kids instead of the elevator when you go to a doctor's appointment, by walking on errands together instead of always driving, or by raking leaves with your kids instead of relying on a leaf blower or a lawn service to do the work. If being physically active is a regular part of your day and your child sees this, you really don't have to say much about it. Once again, actions speak louder than words do—and your child will get the healthy message by seeing you in action.

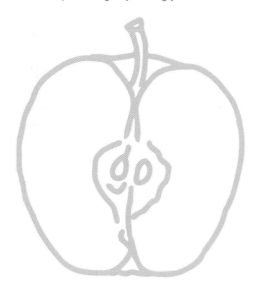

How can I let my child get enough active playtime under proper supervision?

Depending on the age of your child, you may be able to sign him or her up to participate in activity classes (for example, dance, gymnastics, or martial arts) or sports leagues (such as basketball, soccer, baseball, or tennis) that are well supervised by trained professionals. It's best to have your children enrolled in at least one movement-oriented activity that appeals to them. In between those structured activities, you can take your kids and their friends to the park or for a walk in the neighborhood after work, or you can take breaks to dance or play ring-around-the-rosy in the living room while you're making dinner. Then you can spend the better part of each weekend day doing something physical, such as cross-country skiing, canoeing, in-line (or ice) skating, bike riding, or hiking. Remember, being active doesn't require that your child do something sweat-inducing or difficult; just moving at a moderate to vigorous pace and using his or her muscles will make a difference. So take advantage of every opportunity for movement.

A Child's Exercise Rx
How much is enough?

Children and adolescents, ages 6 to 17, should do 60 minutes of moderate- or vigorous-intensity physical activity per day, according to the latest guidelines issued by the U.S. Department of Health and Human Services. It doesn't have to be nonstop; it can be intermittent, even cumulative, throughout the day, though it's best done in bouts of 15 minutes or more.

Most of the movement should be aerobically active (such as running, skipping, dancing, or jumping rope), though part of it should also include muscle-strengthening activities (such as climbing trees or playground equipment) and bone-building activities (anything involving impact with the ground–basketball, tennis, hop-scotch, or jumping rope). In fact, during the day, extended periods of inactivity—meaning sedentary stints of longer than two hours at a time—are actually discouraged for children.

Yet many children in the United States are coming up short when it comes to physical activity. Only 35 percent of kids engaged in 60 minutes of any kind of physical activity that raised their heart and breathing rates for part of the time on five of the previous seven days, according to the latest survey by the Centers for Disease Control and Prevention (CDC). That's the same percentage of kids who managed to watch TV for three or more hours on an average school day.

The reality is, participation in physical activity often declines steeply throughout childhood, especially among adolescent girls. In a study involving nearly 2,400 girls, researchers at the University of Pittsburgh School of Medicine found that between the ages of 9 or 10 and 18 or 19, there was a median of a 100 percent decline in leisure-time physical activity among African-American girls and a 64 percent decline among Caucasian girls; by the age of 16 or 17, 56 percent of the African-American girls and 31 percent of the Caucasian girls reported no regular physical activity whatsoever. And when you look at the big picture, what typically happens with children is fairly startling: Research has found that from first through twelfth grade, kids' levels of moderate-to-vigorous physical activity drop from an average of nearly 200 minutes per week to just 50, though boys tend to be more active than girls.

Participation in physical activity often declines steeply throughout childhood, especially among adolescent girls.

So What's Stopping You?

When it comes to regularly moving more in your day-to-day life, research has found that the barriers women have (or think they have) to being physically active are fairly consistent. These include time constraints, fatigue, health problems, absence of childcare, lack of support or encouragement, financial challenges, and lack of motivation or interest. Meanwhile, research from the University of Guelph in Ontario, Canada, found that among adolescent girls the main perceived barriers to participating in physical activities were lack of time, involvement in technology-related activities, the influence of peers and parents, concerns about safety, inaccessibility of facilities and/or the cost of using them, competition, and body-centered concerns.

THE TRUTH IS, all these barriers can be overcome with careful planning and creativity. Here are some ways around each of them:

☆ Getting physical doesn't have to require a huge time investment. You can make it a multitasking activity by spending time with friends or family members to make it social or by walking to do errands.

☆ Moving your body regularly can actually relieve fatigue and help improve many health problems, ranging from type 2 diabetes and depression to high blood pressure and joint stiffness.

☆ If child care is an issue, you can participate in physical activities with your kids or join a kid-friendly gym.

☆ If you enlist the support of your whole family, it will become much easier and more motivating to make fitness a family affair.

Can activities such as ballet or martial arts help kids get and stay fit as well as traditional sports do?

Absolutely. In fact, they're the complete package when it comes to fitness: Not only do they offer an aerobic workout, as they alternate between moderate and more vigorous movements, but dance and martial arts offer the additional benefits of enhancing the strength and flexibility of lots of different muscles. (This, in turn, helps their bodies start using fat as fuel instead of storing it.) Which means that your kids get a tremendous bang for their exercise buck with these activities. But you don't need to tell them that. Just let them think they're having fun and getting better at something they enjoy—that's a big enough payoff in their minds.

☆ Moving and playing don't have to be expensive; walking is free, and so are many other activities at a local park or community center.

☆ If you exercise with a buddy or family member and take proper precautions (by warming up and increasing your workouts appropriately), safety concerns can be taken care of.

☆ If you limit your kids' screen time to a maximum of two hours per day, that opens up plenty of free time in which you and your kids can get moving.

☆ Getting physical can also help your kids feel better about their bodies; as they get stronger and discover new things their bodies can do, they'll begin to focus more on their bodies as instruments of power, instead of simply their appearance.

Give Yourself an Attitude Check

If you want to help your kids develop a lasting love of movement, it's wise to do some self-reflection to tap into hidden attitudes you may be harboring about being physically active. To do that, consider the following questions:

1. Do you often tell your children to go outside and play? If so, do you ever go with them?

2. Do you make going to the gym or doing exercise of any kind sound like an unpleasant chore?

3. Are you typically critical or upbeat about your own performance when trying a new physical activity for the first time?

4. When watching sports on TV, do you comment mostly on how an athlete performs or mostly on what he or she looks like?

5. Do you often compare your own physical performance to other people's in an exercise class?

6. Do you often make excuses for not exercising—saying that you don't have the time or energy, for example—or find other reasons why you can't get the level of physical activity you know you should?

7. Do you have a double standard when it comes to physical activity for yourself and your children (expecting them to do it but not expecting yourself to, for example)?

8. Do you tend to make life as easy as possible by relying on labor-saving devices or time-saving measures that allow you to avoid opportunities for movement?

9. When you're stressed out, upset, or anxious, are you more likely to use exercise as a way to discharge those unpleasant feelings or to rely on comfort foods to soothe your raw emotions?

10. Are there considerable discrepancies in the fitness levels between you, your spouse, and/or your children?

Thinking about these questions will help you get a feeling for what you've been thinking, saying, and doing when it comes to getting physical and encouraging your kids to do the same. Then you can decide if you're sending your children the messages about moving and playing that you really want them to be receiving. Many smart moms often make mistakes when it comes to talking about movement or exercise with their kids. And the truth is, for better or worse, the way you talk to your child about physical activity can inspire him to get moving—or not.

The Power of Play

To raise physically active kids and help them achieve a healthy weight, you'll want to pay close attention to the language you use as well as the opportunities you create for moving and playing. The first rule: Don't call it "exercise." The word might sound okay to you, but it can make physical activity sound boring and repetitive—like an unpleasant chore—to kids. And when it comes right down to it, kids are motivated by fun, so it's important to make physical activity sound like play, not work. So instead of saying, "Let's go get some exercise," you might say, "Let's go outside and play," "Let's get some fresh air and have an adventure," or "Let's put on some music and have a dance party in the living room." Any activity that sounds festive, free-spirited, whimsical, or playful is bound to appeal to your kids.

Remember, too, kids generally have lots of energy, and doing something physical—whether it's climbing and swinging at the playground, taking the dog for a walk, or jumping rope with other kids from the neighborhood—is a great way for them to run off excess energy, especially after they've spent long hours sitting in a classroom. Given the opportunity, most kids will seize the chance to become movers and shakers—they naturally love the way movement feels, though they may need a little encouragement to bring out these inherent instincts if they've grown accustomed to more sedentary pursuits. In other words, what they need most is a time and place in which they can run, jump, climb, and play to their heart's content.

Again, it helps when both you and your partner are involved in the fitness equation. Researchers at the University of Minnesota found that parental encouragement to be active was associated with increased physical activity among male and female adolescents five years later—but, interestingly, the teens appeared to be especially influenced by the parent of the same sex in this respect. In other words, the girls were especially influenced by their mom's encouragement, while the boys were influenced by their dad's

Watch Your Mouth, Mom!

Take a moment to think about how you speak about exercise.

★ Do you make exercising sound like a bore and a chore when you talk about having to go to the gym?

★ Are you operating with a double standard when it comes to expecting your kids to be physically active while you say that you don't have the time, energy, or inclination to exercise?

★ Do you talk about the benefits of being physically active while relying on your car to do things you could easily do on foot?

Do your best to watch your language and be consistent with the rules. Not only will you boost the likelihood that both you and your kids will get more activity in, but your kids will respect you more in the long run.

Who's Doing What in the Way of Physical Activity?

In a recent online survey, 448 current and past Weight Watchers members with children under age 18 living at home were asked to 'fess up about how often they exercise. It turns out that approximately half of these moms exercise a few times per week or daily—mostly by walking, going to the gym, doing weight training, or exercising to videos—though 24 percent exercise less than once a week. Some of the other things they reported include:

☆ Moms who need to lose more than 10 pounds tend to exercise less frequently, whereas those who have a regular exercise routine are more likely to have good or excellent eating habits.

☆ More than half of the women—54 percent, to be precise—feel guilty for not engaging in physical activity more often.

☆ For the most part, these women say their kids are more physically active than they are; only 21 percent say the whole family is active.

support and encouragement. So try to participate in your child's sporting or recreational life as much as possible, because your involvement could help ensure your child's continued success with it.

Indeed, the best strategies for helping your kids develop healthy habits really do start with you and your behavior and the approach you take toward family fitness. For starters, it's up to you to take charge of your family's schedule and help manage your children's free time in a way that's firm and supportive but not overly strict or domineering—to take an authoritative (but not authoritarian) approach. That may mean setting house rules for when it's active playtime and when TV watching is permissible, or deciding when it makes the most sense for your child to get physical on any given day. After all, flexibility is a must if you want physical activity to be a regular part of your and your child's life, because every day can present different challenges in the way of homework and other things that need to be attended to. In addition, it helps if you, as a parent, do the following:

☆ **Cheer them on.** Psyching kids up to try new sports or physical activities—by giving them a pep talk—and praising their efforts (not just their performance) can help a child stay motivated to stick with those challenges and try new ones. Cheering them on can also help boost their self-efficacy, helping them develop a belief that they really do have the will and the way to do a particular activity. In one study, researchers at Kansas State University found that changes in self-efficacy were associated with positive changes in physical activity among middle-school students. (And if you have some doubts about whether your child can succeed at a new physical task, hide them and cheer him on anyway. Research at Miami University in Ohio found that parental beliefs related to their children's physical competence were significantly related to how much their kids participated in moderate to vigorous physical activities.)

☆ **Don't make couch potato comments.** The truth is, kids thrive on attention, whether it's positive or negative, so it's a mistake to comment verbally on their sedentary behavior. Your kids will either repeat the behavior in the future or turn a deaf ear to your criticisms. A better bet: If your kids are vegging out on the couch and you want them to get physical, simply try to redirect them—by firmly telling them to go play hopscotch or ball, for example. Once they do it, praise them for their positive actions so that you'll promote a repeat performance in the future.

☆ **Encourage them to hang out with active kids.** Kids often gravitate toward like-minded kids in their friendships, and this is true when it comes to physical activity, too. If your child doesn't naturally do this, you can gently steer him or her in the right direction by explaining that it's nice to have different types of friends—friends to chill out with, friends to confide in, friends to do certain hobbies with, friends to play sports with, and so on. In a recent study, researchers at the University of Bristol in the United Kingdom found that friendships played a key role in physical activity participation among 10- and 11-year-old kids. Besides providing the motivation to participate in physical activities together, friends also modeled being active, provided verbal encouragement, and made the whole experience more enjoyable for each other.

☆ **Send them outside—and go with them.** Just spending more time outside fosters physical activity, whether it's walking, biking, or playing active games in your yard or at the park. Research suggests that most kids don't spend enough time outside these days—a phenomenon, dubbed "nature-deficit disorder," that can have lasting effects on a child's physical and emotional development, including increasing his risk of developing weight problems and depression. Once you get into the great outdoors, even if it's just in your neighborhood, you can go on a nature scavenger hunt together, in which you look for heart-shaped rocks, V-shaped sticks, colorful leaves, and the like. Or you can play "I Spy" as you walk. Anything that combines movement and fun is fair game and will appeal to kids.

☆ **Do active chores together.** Walk to the mailbox to send a letter. Rake the leaves in your yard. Wash the car by hand. Or toil together in the garden. Your kids won't see this as work; they'll see it as fun or as a pleasant way to spend time with you. And you'll be achieving two goals at once—taking care of household responsibilities and sneaking some movement into everyone's day.

☆ **Swap active duty with neighbors.** Since many parents can't always take their kids to the park on a sunny afternoon, it's a good idea to trade

If a child isn't athletic, what are some other options for physical activity?

First, it's important to figure out whether your child really isn't the least bit athletic or simply doesn't like the idea of playing on a team. If it's the latter, there are plenty of individual, goal-based sports—tennis, swimming, biking, running, golf, gymnastics, weight lifting, and so on—that emphasize personal achievement rather than team-work. With these, the goal is to do the very best you can so that you can move up the ranks or simply improve your personal best. It may be worth letting your child try his or her hand (and feet and more) at some of these activities. Research suggests that overweight children may have a better experience with individual goal-based physical ac-tivities than with competitive team sports, particularly when first launching a weight-management plan. But if your child is truly turned off by sports, be sensitive to his feelings and personality and try steering him in the direction of active recreational activities (such as bike riding or horseback rid-ing), artistic pursuits (dance, tai chi, karate, or other martial arts, for example), or mind-body forms of exercise (including yoga and Pilates). One or more of these is bound to appeal to your child.

off with neighbors you trust: If you take their kids once a week, they can take yours another day. Or identify a few neighborhood friends who have backyards your kids can play in with their kids. This way, you'll be doubling your kids' opportunities for playing actively outside—and you'll be providing them with playmates, too.

☆ **Consider joining a gym that has kids' programs.** More and more gyms throughout the country are treating fitness as a family affair by offering swimming, basketball, dance, tennis, and other classes and workshops that cater to kids 5 and up. Think of it as one-stop shopping: You and your kids can work out and have fun at the same time and place.

☆ **Plan family outings that include movement on the weekends.** Take a trip to a nature center or a petting zoo. Go apple-, berry-, or pumpkin-picking together. Go bowling or to a laser tag center in inclement weather. During warmer months, play miniature golf or take a trip to a water park. Your kids are bound to love any of these activities—and you'll be moving and enjoying yourselves as a family.

☆ **Take a trip down memory lane.** Make a point of talking about active games and activities that you and your spouse loved when you were kids, such as playing kickball, badminton, kick the can, croquet, and the like. This can help spark your kids' interest in trying these games and activities. Once you've piqued their curiosity, encourage them to invite a bunch of friends over and teach them how to play these games on a weekend afternoon or after dinner one evening.

☆ **Walk them to school.** Or drive part of the way, then walk the rest. Either way, both of you will sneak in some movement at the beginning of your day, before you each sit at a desk or table for the next several hours. This also provides a good opportunity to catch up conversationally on what's going on in each other's lives.

☆ **Consider getting a dog.** Several studies suggest that dog owners get more exercise than non-dog-owners do. And in a study involving 281 children ages 5 and 6 and 864 children between the ages of 10 and 12, researchers at Deakin University in Australia found that the odds of being overweight were 50 percent lower among younger children who had a dog. The researchers concluded, "It is important that families with a dog are encouraged to walk or play with it regularly." If you really can't accommodate a dog in your home, consider letting your kids do some dog walking for friends or neighbors.

☆ **Provide incentives.** In a perfect world, movement would be its own reward. But while you're helping your child become more physically active, it helps to give positive reinforcement in the form of rewards—perhaps some new exercise clothes or sports gear or a visit to a local attraction (such as a facility with a cool climbing wall) after achieving a certain goal. Offering up these incentives will motivate your child to stick with the program and give her something to look forward to while she's developing an exercise habit.

☆ **Praise their efforts.** Just as hearing positive verbal feedback can be a strong motivator for a child to stay active, the opposite is true, too: Hearing criticism or negative comments about their sports performance can discourage them from sticking with it. So recognize your child's progress in mastering or learning new skills, make gentle suggestions for how to improve, and encourage him or her to apply newly developed skills to other activities he or she would like to try. With some subtle prodding and lots of compliments from you, your child will develop a can-do spirit and a positive, open-minded attitude toward being physically active in a variety of ways.

☆ **Let your kids have a say.** Don't just choose their physical activities for them; let them tell you which sports they're interested in trying or pursuing or what kinds of movement-related classes they'd like to join. Just because Dad loved playing soccer when he was a kid, that doesn't mean your son will. And just because you loved ballet, that doesn't mean your daughter will share your enthusiasm. It's important to help your kids discover activities they truly enjoy—and to respect their individual preferences—so that they'll be more likely to stick with them for the long haul. The bottom line: If it's not fun, your kids just won't do it on a regular basis. For kids, the fun factor is essential.

Inside Options

Since you can't control the weather, it's a good idea to stock up on active games for indoor play. Depending on the ages of your children, this might involve filling a plastic tub with balls or rings, batons, Hula-hoops, jump ropes, kid-size hand weights or stretch bands, a hopscotch mat, active games such as Twister, ball-toss games, a Velcro dartboard, or an indoor basketball hoop. That way, kids can run and play inside on a cold or rainy day.

You also may want to consider investing in some of the more active video games, such as Dance Dance Revolution or Wii Sports. By using fast-paced dance sequences or simulating the movements in boxing, tennis, baseball, bowling, or golf, these games get players off the couch and moving more of their bodies than just their hands. In fact, research suggests that playing activity-promoting video games can push a person's calorie-burning potential and heart rate into the aerobic workout zone. Alternatively, you might consider getting some family-friendly exercise videos or DVDs.

Ten Healthy Messages to Send Your Kids About Moving

What to Say, What to Role-Model

Here are ten things to remember yourself and to tell your kids to help them develop or maintain healthy movement habits.

1. **Physical activity is one of the best stress-busters around.** Whether you take a walk when you're upset or you climb the monkey bars at the playground after a tough day at school, doing something physical will help you blow off steam, decompress, and boost your mood.

2. **Moving simply feels good.** When your body is in motion, you can bask in the freedom of movement, exploring the space around you and stretching or flexing muscles that feel stiff or underused.

3. **A strong, fit body is a healthy body.** Emphasizing this truism helps take the focus off weight and appearance and put it squarely on health and well-being, where it rightly belongs.

4. **Getting physical can help you do better in school.** Tell your kids about research suggesting that regular physical activity can enhance their attention and concentration in school—and perhaps even boost their performance in school.

5. **Playing sports or running around with friends is a fun way to spend time together.** You can talk, goof around, and have a good time together while you're on the move. Doing something social doesn't require sitting still.

6. **Being physically active will help your skin and hair look healthy.** This perk may resonate with adolescent girls in particular. You can chalk these benefits up to the fact that exercise enhances blood flow to the skin and scalp.

7. **Be proud of what your body can do.** When your child begins to celebrate his or her physical accomplishments, your child will see his or her body in a whole new light—a powerful, action-oriented one, not just an appearance-based one.

8. **Running around in the afternoon can help you sleep better at night.** The connection may sound surprising to kids, but it really exists. With older kids, you can explain that being physically active causes body temperature to rise during and right after a workout, but then it will fall a few hours later, which puts your body and mind in the mood to snooze.

9. **Participating in sports is even more fun than watching them.** Why be just a spectator when you can be a participant? Sure, it's fun to watch professional or college sports, but it's also a blast to see what you can do on the court or field.

10. **Moving when you're tired can boost your energy.** It may sound counterintuitive, so you might explain that when kids feel tired after sitting at school all day, running, climbing, or jumping can actually rejuvenate their spirits and energy, leaving them feeling refreshed.

Get Moving with Your Kids

The key is to do enjoyable physical activities together so that it doesn't feel like a chore to either of you. It simply feels like play. Here are fun-filled activities to do with kids of every age.

BABIES. Go for a brisk walk or jog with your baby in a stroller or baby jogger; sign up for Baby Boot Camp or some kind of Stroller-cize class in your area; do a baby-and-me yoga DVD; go for a hike with your baby in a backpack-style carrier; take an aqua exercise class with your baby in a heated pool.

TODDLERS AND PRESCHOOLERS. Put on some music and dance in your living room; go for a bike ride with your tot in a child seat; fly a kite together, running as you do it; go sledding or head off on a nature walk together; actively play on the climbing or swinging equipment with your youngster at the playground.

SCHOOL-AGE KIDS. Kick a soccer ball together; take a parent-child karate class; play tennis or racquetball; go skiing or ice-skating together; play tag in your backyard; go rowing or canoeing or kayaking together; jump rope with your child and her friends (double Dutch, anyone?).

TWEENS AND TEENS. Go in-line skating together; play basketball or volleyball; take a funk or street jam or ballroom dance class or participate in a Spinning class together; play golf (or Frisbee golf), walking the course as you go; go someplace where you can do a climbing wall together.

Coaching 101

Kids aren't small adults. In fact, they are wired differently than adults in a number of ways: They don't have the endurance or the stamina to engage in physical activities for as long as you can, their bones and joints aren't as mature and stable as yours are, and their metabolic systems are better suited for short periods of vigorous movement than long, continuous workouts. In fact, before they reach puberty, kids just don't have the circulating hormones that would enable them to, say, walk briskly for 20 to 30 minutes at a time. And because kids have more fast-twitch muscles than slow-twitch ones, they're better suited to power sports, stop-and-go activities, and intense bursts of movement—such as in a game of tag. What's more, kids run out of glucose (fuel) in their muscles much more quickly than adults do, which is why it's a good idea for them to switch from playing of-

What are some physical things kids can do indoors during the colder months?

First of all, just because it's cold outside, that doesn't mean your kids have to stay inside. Kids love to play in the snow, and building snowmen and going sledding are great forms of physical activity. Even if it's just chilly but there's no snow, you can take a walk or play at the park, then come in for some (low-fat) hot chocolate to help everyone warm up.

But if you're set on staying inside, there are plenty of active options available. Many community centers open their gyms for free play during the winter months, and there are indoor playgrounds in many suburban areas. Plus there are often indoor activity programs or classes at religious institutions and other community organizations. You can also set up active fun-filled activities in your own home; try creating an obstacle course where kids have to jump on cushions, climb over tables, crawl through Hula-hoops, and so on. Active board games such as Twister or free-play games such as freeze dance are perennial favorites among kids. Or you can buy Hula-hoops, juggling balls, stretch bands, or a mini trampoline to use in a playroom or basement. Then let them play their hearts out.

fense to defense periodically in soccer, for instance. The bottom line: Kids really do need to vary the pace of their physical activities for all sorts of physiological reasons.

Since children's bodies are still growing and developing, you'll want to help your kids engage in physical activities in a way that's appropriate for their ages and stages of life. For the sake of their development of muscle strength and coordination, it's best for kids to cross-train—to participate in a variety of activities rather than doing the same one all the time. In fact, the current thinking is that kids shouldn't start intense training in any given sport until they are at least 12 years old. Sticking with variety will also help kids avoid mental and physical burnout and overuse injuries that can occur with doing the same sports over and over again, day after day.

If your child has been inactive until now, start slowly and build up from there. Try to discourage your child from increasing the duration or intensity of an activity by more than about 10 percent per week, to prevent injuries and burnout. Encourage your children to listen to their bodies—to slow down if they're overexerting themselves or experiencing discomfort and to speed up or push themselves harder if an activity feels too easy. Most of all, be patient when it comes to your child's progress. It takes a child three months to increase his or her fitness level by 25 percent, which means that it can take a year to reach his or her true potential. Celebrate all the progress along the way because every bit of improvement in physical fitness really does count.

By making physical activity a family affair, your kids will grow up thinking this is just a normal, enjoyable part of spending time together as a family. It may not happen overnight, especially if you've all been relatively sedentary in the past. But these changes will become easier over time, especially since kids are so highly adaptable and such quick learners. Once again, practice makes perfect, and they'll be going with the flow (of movement) before you know it.

Just be sure to take an equal-opportunity approach to physical activity so that everyone in the family gets plenty of movement, whether or not they have weight issues. If one of your children is naturally slim and another is putting on excess pounds, you should be encouraging both kids to take part in plenty of active play. Similarly, if one child is a natural-born athlete and another is less coordinated, it's important to find recreational activities that everyone can do comfortably (such as bike riding, hiking, or swimming). Getting physical shouldn't take on a tone of punishment or exclusivity; it should be something that everyone is encouraged to do to feel good and be healthy and fit.

Ultimately, when you participate in physical activities with your kids instead of just watching them, everybody wins. You and your children will be moving more, you'll be setting a healthy example for your kids, and your presence will encourage them to try new physical activities and stick with those they enjoy. Plus, you'll be spending precious quality time together as parent and child, which is what kids crave most in this world.

What's more, sticking with these get-moving strategies will help create a lifestyle that promotes a healthy family unit, as well as robust health and a weight that is healthy

The Sporting Life, Safely

By some estimates, roughly 50 percent of the injuries children experience during sports participation could be prevented if only the right precautions were taken. This includes using the proper equipment, maintaining safe playing surfaces, having adequate adult supervision and well-qualified coaches, and making sure your child has had the proper training and conditioning to participate in a given sport. Here are sport-specific safety moves you'll want to keep in mind.

Baseball and softball

- Use breakaway bases to minimize the risk of ankle injuries.
- Have kids wear snug-fitting batting helmets with a face guard.
- Limit the number of throws and teach proper throwing technique to decrease elbow and shoulder injuries.

Basketball

- Have your child wear a mouth guard.
- Invest in well-fitting, high-quality, supportive high-top shoes.
- Be sure the coach has kids perform conditioning, strengthening, and warm-up exercises before playing games.

Biking

- Insist that your child wear a hard-shell bike helmet that fits correctly.
- Make sure the bike is an appropriate size and is well maintained.
- Be sure your child understands and follows the rules of the road before letting her ride off the sidewalk.

Football

- Make sure your child's helmet, shoulder pads, mouth guard, and other equipment fit correctly and are in good condition.
- Let him play only under the supervision of an experienced, safety-conscious coach who teaches proper techniques for tackling and falling.
- Have your child join a team and league with kids who are matched for skill level and size.

In-line skating

- Insist that your child wear a helmet, wrist guards, elbow pads, knee pads, and gloves.
- Encourage her to learn on a smooth, flat surface.
- Ask her to take it slowly until she can skate with good control and stop precisely.

Soccer

- Make sure your child wears well-fitting shin guards and cleats.
- Check the field's condition to be sure it's free of holes, rocks, and other hazards.
- Insist that kids be taught how to head the ball properly (with the forehead)—and only in moderation.

and appropriate for each member of the family. Think of yourself as an agent of change, as the driving force for launching these health-promoting lifestyle adjustments. After all, to a large extent your health and weight—as well as your kids'—are tied to the lifestyle choices you make on a daily basis, and the eating and movement habits your kids develop are likely to stay with them for life. In a sense, these changes will serve as a long-lasting gift for the whole family. Help family members embrace this concept, then enlist everyone's involvement so that healthy living, eating, and moving really do become an enduring family affair. The benefits to each family member will never end.

How do I get a kid who prefers to watch TV to start moving?

Often children watch TV or play on the computer because they can't think of something else to do. In other words, screen time becomes a default activity when they're bored or tired. One way to get a child moving is to give three choices, none of which involves TV but two of which aren't appealing and one of which is physically active. You might tell your child he can unload the dishwasher, vacuum the living room, or jump rope (or shoot hoops or some such) for 10 minutes, and let him take his pick; chances are, jumping rope (or shooting hoops) will suddenly seem appealing. Simply by turning off the TV and giving your child active alternatives, you'll be (gently) pushing him in the right direction. But if your child really is tired and you're inclined to let him watch TV, you can strike a deal: At every commercial break he will do jumping jacks, push-ups, or sit-ups.

It can also help to reorder a child's after-school routine. Instead of having him do homework right away, give your child a glass of water, then send him outside to play ball or tag for at least 30 minutes. Besides ensuring that your child sneaks in some movement, this gives his brain a chance to recharge after the school day and before tackling the homework challenge. Later, he can watch TV if time allows.

Once regular physical activity becomes a family habit, you can use it to reinforce the healthy eating habits you're also trying to instill in your kids—and vice versa. You might point out, for example, the importance of choosing nutrient-rich foods to serve as high-octane fuel for your kids' activities so they'll have plenty of energy to keep moving and grooving. On the flip side, you might also point out that when you've been running around, expending lots of energy, it feels good to replenish your body with healthy foods and lots of good, old-fashioned H_2O.

Wrap Up: Setting Goals

Now that you've discovered how your approach to cultivating more play and movement in your family's life can have a lasting effect on your kids and what they really need in the way of physical activity, it's time to set some goals.

Think about a few specific strategies you'd like to implement in both the short term and the long term to upgrade your family's physical activity habits, keeping an eye on what's feasible given your family's busy schedule. Taking these steps should help you become a more effective provider, protector, enforcer, and role model when it comes to helping your kids develop a lifelong love of movement.

Something to try this week: _____

_____

_____

_____

Something to try this month: _____

_____

_____

_____

Something to try in the near future: _____

_____

_____

_____

Watermelon Cake with Raspberry
Sauce, page 211

In the Kitchen

Delicious, fun, and healthy—our recipe collection is here to help you and your family enjoy mealtimes and good food together. We provide expert advice and tips to help kids get involved with some of the preparation of these easy home-cooked meals and to start them on a lifelong, healthy relationship with eating well.

BREAKFASTS & BRUNCHES

Brunch Strata

1 onion, chopped

1 red bell pepper, chopped

½ pound fully cooked low-fat chicken sausage, diced

1 (8-ounce) package cremini mushrooms, halved and sliced

1 teaspoon dried thyme

⅛ teaspoon salt

1 (12-ounce) whole-wheat baguette, cubed

2 cups shredded fat-free cheddar cheese

5 large eggs

1½ cups low-fat (1%) milk

1 tablespoon Dijon mustard

1. Spray a 9 × 13-inch baking dish with nonstick spray.

2. Spray a large nonstick skillet with nonstick spray and set it over medium heat. Add the onion and cook until it begins to soften, about 3 minutes. Add the pepper and sausage and cook until the sausage is lightly browned, about 4 minutes. Add the mushrooms, thyme, and salt and cook until the mushrooms start to brown, about 6 minutes. Scrape into a large bowl and toss with the bread and cheese. Spread the mixture evenly in the baking dish.

3. Whisk the eggs, milk, and mustard together in a medium bowl. Pour evenly over the bread mixture in the dish. Cover and refrigerate at least 2 hours or overnight.

4. Preheat the oven to 350°F. Bake the strata, uncovered, until it is puffed and golden brown, 35–40 minutes. Cool in the pan for 10 minutes before cutting into 8 squares.

PER SERVING (3 × 4-INCH SQUARE): *277 Cal, 8 g Fat, 2 g Sat Fat, 0 g Trans Fat, 162 mg Chol, 927 mg Sod, 30 g Carb, 5 g Fib, 24 g Prot, 381 mg Calc.*

Try it

Stratas are popular brunch dishes because they can be prepared the night before and popped into the oven the next morning, but don't limit yourself: They are also great one-dish dinners. And if you have leftovers, you're in luck; they reheat very well, covered, in a 350°F oven until hot, about 20 minutes.

Mini Mexican Frittatas

toddler friendly

SERVES 6 | PREP 5 minutes | BAKE 20 minutes

4 large eggs

¼ cup low-fat (1%) milk

¼ cup mild salsa

¼ cup shredded reduced-fat cheddar cheese

¼ teaspoon ground cumin

¼ teaspoon salt

1. Preheat the oven to 350°F. Spray the cups of a 6-cup muffin pan lightly with nonstick spray.

2. Whisk the eggs, milk, salsa, cheese, cumin, and salt together in a medium bowl. Ladle the mixture evenly into the muffin cups.

3. Bake until the egg mixture puffs up and the edges are golden brown, about 20 minutes. Remove the pan from the oven, run a butter knife around the edge of each cup, and lift the frittatas out.

PER SERVING (1 FRITTATA): *71 Cal, 5 g Fat, 2 g Sat Fat, 0 g Trans Fat, 145 mg Chol, 218 mg Sod, 2 g Carb, 0 g Fib, 6 g Prot, 63 mg Calc.*

Kids can...

Whisk the frittata ingredients together and help ladle the mixture into the muffin cups.

Cottage Cheese Pancakes

toddler friendly

SERVES 6 | **PREP** 10 minutes | **COOK** 20 minutes

1 cup low-fat cottage cheese

1 cup vanilla low-fat yogurt

3 large eggs

1 teaspoon vanilla extract

1 cup all-purpose flour

⅓ cup whole-wheat flour

1 tablespoon sugar

¼ teaspoon salt

1. Whisk the cottage cheese, yogurt, eggs, and vanilla together in a large bowl. Stir in the all-purpose flour, whole-wheat flour, sugar, and salt.

2. Spray a large nonstick skillet or griddle with nonstick spray and heat over medium heat. Pour the batter by 2-tablespoon measures onto the griddle. Cook until small bubbles just begin to appear on top of the pancakes and they are golden brown underneath, about 2 minutes. Flip and cook until the second side has browned, about 2 minutes longer.

PER SERVING (4 PANCAKES): *207 Cal, 4 g Fat, 1 g Sat Fat, 0 g Trans Fat, 110 mg Chol, 309 mg Sod, 30 g Carb, 1 g Fib, 13 g Prot, 111 mg Calc.*

Smart move

Instead of offering your child a cookie, suggest he or she try one of these healthful pancakes as a treat. If you'd like to warm up leftovers quickly, wrap one or two in a paper towel and microwave on High for 20–30 seconds.

Helping Hands

Every Mom wants her child to develop a healthy attitude toward food, but when it comes to the day-to-day reality of meal planning and eating, it's probably best to keep your expectations realistic. In fact, you're probably thrilled when your child agrees to try a new food or suddenly wants to eat something (anything!) other than plain macaroni. While you can't necessarily dictate your children's food preferences, you can try to expand their food horizons by offering them a wide variety of tastes and textures.

Another way to nudge children toward expanding their food repertoire is to make cooking an enjoyable activity. While most kids are excited about helping out in the kitchen, you need to keep in mind age-appropriate tasks that you can offer them. Some suggestions:

Toddlers (ages 2–4) Young children are developing hand and finger control and are beginning to take pride in following simple directions. They can have fun doing a number of simple kitchen tasks:

- ☆ Rinsing fruits and vegetables and patting them dry
- ☆ Pulling parsley and cilantro leaves off their stems
- ☆ Wiping the counter or table with a sponge or paper towel
- ☆ Tearing lettuce and salad greens into bite-size pieces
- ☆ Peeling the skins from bananas
- ☆ Layering ingredients into sandwiches and over pizzas
- ☆ Sprinkling toppings on casseroles and salads

Kids (ages 5–9) Kids at this age are developing arm and hand strength, mastering counting and simple math, and increasing their attention span. They will enjoy being set to the following tasks:

- ☆ Snipping herbs and leafy vegetables with kids' safety scissors
- ☆ Cutting soft fruits like bananas and strawberries with a plastic knife
- ☆ Stirring, whisking, or sifting ingredients together
- ☆ Measuring out dry and liquid ingredients (work over the sink to catch spills)
- ☆ Juicing lemons or limes
- ☆ Spreading soft foods such as peanut butter on bread or icing on cupcakes
- ☆ Setting the table for dinner

Preteens (ages 10–12) Most preteens can read through a recipe, and with a little supervision (and assistance) from adults can accomplish most simple preparation tasks, including:

- ☆ Slicing soft foods such as mushrooms, zucchini, cheese, and pitted olives
- ☆ Cracking eggs
- ☆ Peeling carrots, cucumbers, and other vegetables with a vegetable peeler
- ☆ Using a box grater to shred cheeses and vegetables
- ☆ Spraying baking pans
- ☆ Opening cans with a can opener
- ☆ Choosing serving plates and garnishing food attractively

Breakfast Berry Sundaes

SERVES 2 | **PREP** 5 minutes | **NO COOK**

8 strawberries, hulled and sliced

1 cup vanilla low-fat yogurt

2 tablespoons granola

1 banana, peeled and sliced

½ cup blueberries

Using two parfait or other glasses, put half the strawberries into each glass and top each with ¼ cup of the yogurt. Layer in the granola, the remaining yogurt, the banana slices, and finally the blueberries.

PER SERVING (1 GLASS): *213 Cal, 3 g Fat, 1 g Sat Fat, 0 g Trans Fat, 6 mg Chol, 91 mg Sod, 42 g Carb, 4 g Fib, 8 g Prot, 226 mg Calc.*

Smart move

What's so important about colorful food? Lots! The different colors of fruits and vegetables represent different combinations of nutrients, so using the rainbow not only makes your dishes look appealing, like this beautiful sundae, but also supports a balanced diet.

Oatmeal Pancakes with Blueberry-Maple Syrup

SERVES 6 | PREP 10 minutes | COOK 20 minutes

1 cup old-fashioned rolled oats

¾ cup whole-wheat pastry flour

¾ cup all-purpose flour

¼ cup ground flaxseed

3 tablespoons sugar

2 teaspoons baking powder

¼ teaspoon salt

2⅓ cups low-fat buttermilk

1 large egg

1½ teaspoons vanilla extract

1 cup blueberries

¼ cup maple syrup

1. Combine the oats, flours, flaxseed, sugar, baking powder, and salt in a large bowl. Whisk the buttermilk, egg, and vanilla together in another bowl. Stir the buttermilk mixture into the flour mixture until blended. Let stand 3 minutes.

2. Spray a large nonstick skillet or griddle with nonstick spray and heat over medium heat. Pour the batter by ¼-cup measures onto the griddle. Cook until small bubbles just begin to appear on top of the pancakes and they are golden brown underneath, about 3 minutes. Flip and cook until the second side has browned, about 2 minutes longer. Combine blueberries and syrup in small saucepan and cook over medium-low heat until warmed. Serve over pancakes.

PER SERVING (3 PANCAKES AND 2½ TABLESPOONS BLUEBERRY SYRUP): *304 Cal, 5 g Fat, 1 g Sat Fat, 0 g Trans Fat, 39 mg Chol, 338 mg Sod, 55 g Carb, 4 g Fib, 11 g Prot, 185 mg Calc.*

Try it

Ground flaxseed, a source of fiber, antioxidants, and omega-3s, is one of the current darlings of the nutritional world. Try adding small amounts to breakfast cereal or baked goods.

Pumpkin Pie Muffins

SERVES 12 | **PREP** 15 minutes | **BAKE** 20 minutes

1 cup all-purpose flour

¾ cup whole-wheat pastry flour

1¼ cups sugar

1¼ teaspoons baking soda

1 teaspoon cinnamon

½ teaspoon salt

½ teaspoon ground nutmeg

½ teaspoon ground cloves

½ cup raisins

2 large eggs, lightly beaten

1 cup canned pumpkin puree

⅓ cup canola oil

⅓ cup water

2 tablespoons raw pumpkin seeds

1. Preheat the oven to 350°F. Spray the cups of a 12-cup muffin pan lightly with nonstick spray.

2. Sift the all-purpose flour, whole-wheat flour, sugar, baking soda, cinnamon, salt, nutmeg, and cloves into a large bowl; stir in the raisins. Beat the eggs, pumpkin puree, oil, and water together in another bowl. Add the pumpkin mixture to the flour mixture and stir just until blended.

3. Spoon the batter into the muffin cups, filling each about two-thirds full. Sprinkle with the pumpkin seeds. Bake until a toothpick inserted into a muffin comes out clean, about 20 minutes. Cool in the pan on a rack for 10 minutes; remove the muffins from the pan and serve warm or cool completely on the rack.

PER SERVING (1 MUFFIN): *235 Cal, 8 g Fat, 1 g Sat Fat, 0 g Trans Fat, 35 mg Chol, 241 mg Sod, 40 g Carb, 2 g Fib, 4 g Prot, 20 mg Calc.*

Kids can...

Sift the dry ingredients together, then sprinkle the pumpkin seeds evenly over the tops of the unbaked muffins.

SNACKS AT HOME & ON THE GO

Edamame Dip with Crackers and Carrots

SERVES 4 | PREP 5 minutes | COOK 5 minutes

1 cup frozen shelled edamame

4 ounces silken tofu

1 scallion, trimmed and sliced

1 garlic clove, chopped

1 tablespoon lemon juice

1½ teaspoons olive oil

½ teaspoon ground cumin

¼ teaspoon honey

¼ teaspoon salt

12 whole-wheat crackers

12 carrot or other vegetable sticks

Cook the edamame according to the package directions. Place them in a food processor along with the tofu, scallion, garlic, lemon juice, oil, cumin, honey, and salt. Process until smooth, 1–2 minutes, scraping down the side of the bowl as needed. Serve with the crackers and vegetable sticks.

PER SERVING (ABOUT ¼ CUP DIP, 3 CRACKERS, AND 3 CARROT STICKS): *169 Cal, 7 g Fat, 1 g Sat Fat, 0 g Trans Fat, 0 mg Chol, 264 mg Sod, 18 g Carb, 5 g Fib, 9 g Prot, 78 mg Calc.*

Try it

Edamame, or green soybeans, are a wonderful source of protein, fiber, and isoflavones, and this dip is a great way to introduce them to your family. Also try edamame in soups, stews, stir-fries, salads, and noodle dishes, where their nutty taste, firm texture, and spring-green color can make them more palatable than other beans.

Creamy Broccoli Dip

SERVES 8 | PREP 15 minutes | STEAM 10 minutes

1 broccoli head (about 1 pound), cut into florets

2 teaspoons extra-virgin olive oil

1 onion, chopped

2 garlic cloves, finely chopped

Juice of ½ lemon

2 tablespoons grated Parmesan

2 tablespoons whipped cream cheese

¼ teaspoon salt

1. Put the broccoli in a steamer basket and place in a saucepan over 1 inch of boiling water. Cover the pan tightly and steam until the broccoli is very tender, 6–8 minutes. Cool the broccoli under cold running water and set aside.

2. Meanwhile, in a small nonstick skillet, heat the oil over medium heat. Add the onion and cook until tender, about 5 minutes. Add the garlic and cook about 30 seconds longer.

3. Combine the broccoli, onion mixture, lemon juice, Parmesan, cream cheese, and salt in a food processor and pulse until smooth, adding a few tablespoons of water if the mixture is too thick.

PER SERVING (ABOUT ¼ CUP): *50 Cal, 3 g Fat, 1 g Sat Fat, 0 g Trans Fat, 4 mg Chol, 119 mg Sod, 5 g Carb, 2 g Fib, 3 g Prot, 52 mg Calc.*

Smart move

Whole-wheat crackers and vegetables such as carrot, celery, and cucumber sticks are all healthful dippers, but be sure to ask your kids what veggies they think might taste good with this dip. How about raw zucchini rounds? Snow peas? Radishes? Baby corn? Getting kids involved in food choices is a helpful way to steer them toward healthier options.

Perfect for Toddlers

Bye-bye, baby food! It's exciting to watch your toddler's culinary world expand day by day, food by food. But it's also easy to fall into a rut, relying too heavily on sweet or salty snack foods, or buying expensive prepared foods aimed at easing parental anxieties about processed grains and additives. The following simple, family-friendly recipes are our top suggestions for helping you feed your toddler at home and on the go; just look for our toddler-friendly icon. *toddler friendly* ☺

Mini Mexican Frittatas (page 108)

Cottage Cheese Pancakes (page 109)

Breakfast Berry Sundaes (page 111)

Spinach Snack Bites (page 121)

Cheesy Mini Muffins (page 122)

Smart Bars (page 125)

Honey-Mustard Turkey Strips (page 130)

Stoplight Pita Sandwiches (page 134)

Grilled Cheese Triangles (page 142)

Turkey and Rice "Mice" (page 168)

Crumb-Topped Mac 'n' Cheese (page 192)

Personal Pizzas (page 195)

Butternut Squash Puree (page 204)

Frozen Fruit Pops (page 214)

Always be patient with young eaters: Studies have shown that children may need to be exposed to a new food as many as 14 times over the course of several months before they begin to accept it. So concentrate on offering them a wide variety of healthful foods, early and often.

And remember, toddlers are notoriously uneven in their eating habits, seemingly ravenous one day, sparing in appetite the next. Unless your pediatrician advises otherwise, it may be more important to focus on the nutritional quality of what your toddler eats and less on the quantity.

Note that although we include nutritional information for all recipes and give **POINTS**® values on page 226, unless instructed to do so by a pediatrician, parents need not count the number of calories or **POINTS** values their children consume.

Spinach Snack Bites

toddler friendly

SERVES 24 | PREP 10 minutes | BAKE 45 minutes

2 (10-ounce) packages frozen spinach, thawed and squeezed dry

8 ounces feta cheese, crumbled

1 cup shredded reduced-fat sharp cheddar cheese

4 large eggs

2 large egg whites

1. Preheat the oven to 350°F. Spray a 9 × 13-inch baking dish with nonstick spray.

2. Stir the spinach, feta, cheddar, eggs, and egg whites together in a large bowl. Pour into the baking dish. Bake until the mixture is set and the top is golden brown, about 45 minutes. Cool slightly, then cut into 24 squares. Serve warm or cold.

PER SERVING (1 SQUARE): *59 Cal, 4 g Fat, 2 g Sat Fat, 0 g Trans Fat, 47 mg Chol, 178 mg Sod, 2 g Carb, 1 g Fib, 5 g Prot, 110 mg Calc.*

Kids can...

Crumble the feta with their hands or a fork. Older kids might try separating the egg whites from the yolks—just do each one over a fresh bowl, and expect a few do-overs!

Cheesy Mini Muffins

toddler friendly

SERVES 24 | PREP 15 minutes | BAKE 20 minutes

1 cup all-purpose flour

¼ cup whole-wheat flour

¼ cup oat bran

1 teaspoon baking powder

1 teaspoon Italian seasoning

½ teaspoon salt

1 large egg

1 cup shredded reduced-fat Jarlsberg or cheddar cheese

¾ cup milk

2 tablespoons canola oil

1 large carrot, shredded

1. Preheat the oven to 350°F. Spray the cups of a 24-cup mini muffin pan with nonstick spray.

2. Stir the all-purpose flour, whole-wheat flour, oat bran, baking powder, Italian seasoning, and salt together in a large bowl. Whisk the egg, cheese, milk, oil, and carrot together in another bowl. Pour the cheese mixture over the flour mixture and use a rubber spatula to fold them together.

3. Scoop about 1 tablespoon of the batter into each muffin cup. Bake until a toothpick inserted in the center of a muffin comes out clean, 18–20 minutes. Cool in the pan on a rack 5 minutes; remove the muffins from the pan and cool completely on the rack.

PER SERVING (1 MINI MUFFIN): *60 Cal, 3 g Fat, 1 g Sat Fat, 0 g Trans Fat, 13 mg Chol, 112 mg Sod, 6 g Carb, 1 g Fib, 3 g Prot, 51 mg Calc.*

Smart move

Having a few healthful, portable snacks in your arsenal can help keep your family's eating habits on track. If you take some of these delicious mini muffins along on outings, for instance, you'll be less likely to have to rely on unhealthful snack alternatives.

Pineapple Crush Smoothies

SERVES 3 | PREP 5 minutes | NO COOK

1 ripe banana, peeled and cut into chunks

1 (8-ounce) can crushed pineapple in juice

½ cup plain low-fat yogurt

½ cup orange juice

1 tablespoon honey

5 ice cubes

1. Place the banana on a plate and put it in the freezer until hard, about 1 hour.

2. Combine the frozen banana, pineapple with juice, yogurt, orange juice, and honey in a blender and blend on High for 30 seconds. Stop the blender, add the ice cubes and blend until the mixture is smooth and thick. Divide among 3 glasses.

PER SERVING (1 CUP): *148 Cal, 1 g Fat, 0 g Sat Fat, 0 g Trans Fat, 3 mg Chol, 30 mg Sod, 35 g Carb, 2 g Fib, 3 g Prot, 90 mg Calc.*

Smart move

Here's a great way to save bananas that are on their way to being overripe: Peel and slice them, then place in a zip-close freezer bag and store in the freezer. Now you're ready to make a smoothie anytime. If you have leftover smoothie, pour it into an ice-pop mold for a healthful frozen treat.

Smart Bars

toddler friendly

SERVES 32 | PREP 10 minutes | BAKE 20 minutes

1 cup quick-cooking oats

½ cup sunflower seeds

½ cup toasted wheat germ

½ cup dried apricots

½ cup pecan halves

½ cup raisins

½ cup dried cranberries

½ cup instant nonfat dry milk

¼ cup whole-wheat pastry flour

1 teaspoon cinnamon

⅓ cup maple syrup

2 large eggs

1 ripe banana, peeled and cut into chunks

1 teaspoon vanilla extract

1. Preheat the oven to 350ºF. Coat a 9 × 13-inch baking pan with nonstick spray.

2. Combine the oats, sunflower seeds, wheat germ, apricots, pecans, raisins, cranberries, dry milk, flour, and cinnamon in a food processor. Pulse until the mixture is finely chopped. Add the syrup, eggs, banana, and vanilla and pulse until well combined.

3. Transfer the mixture to the pan, wet your fingertips with cool water, and press down to level the surface. Bake until the mixture is golden brown and firm to the touch, about 20 minutes.

4. Cool in the pan and cut into 32 bars.

PER SERVING (1 BAR): *83 Cal, 3 g Fat, 0 g Sat Fat, 0 g Trans Fat, 14 mg Chol, 11 mg Sod, 12 g Carb, 2 g Fib, 3 g Prot, 27 mg Calc.*

Kids can...

Peel the banana, then moisten their hands and use their fingertips to press the bar mixture into the pan as evenly as possible.

LUNCHES & LIGHT MEALS

Quick Quesadillas

SERVES 4 | **PREP** 5 minutes | **COOK** 10 minutes

4 (8-inch) whole-wheat tortillas

4 thin slices prosciutto

4 thin slices pepperjack cheese

4 scallions, thinly sliced

¼ cup chopped cilantro

¼ cup salsa

1. Spray a large grill pan with nonstick spray and place over medium-high heat.

2. Place a tortilla on the counter and cover with one-fourth of the prosciutto and cheese. Sprinkle the bottom half with one-fourth of the scallions and cilantro. Fold the tortilla in half, covering the fillings. Repeat with the remaining tortillas, prosciutto, cheese, scallions, and cilantro.

3. Place 2 quesadillas in the pan and cook, turning once, until the tortillas are browned and the cheese has melted, 2–3 minutes. Repeat with the remaining quesadillas. Cut each quesadilla into 3 even wedges and serve with the salsa on the side.

PER SERVING (1 QUESADILLA AND 1 TABLESPOON SALSA): *165 Cal, 7 g Fat, 3 g Sat Fat, 0 g Trans Fat, 25 mg Chol, 592 mg Sod, 22 g Carb, 3 g Fib, 11 g Prot, 130 mg Calc.*

Smart move

What's so great about making restaurant food, such as quesadillas, at home? Lots! Not only is it fun, but home-cooked food is generally more healthful. Best of all, you can get really creative with the ingredients you use and customize everything to your family's tastes.

Chinese Chicken Salad

SERVES 4 | PREP 20 minutes | NO COOK

1 (1-pound) bag coleslaw mix

3 scallions, sliced

1 (8-ounce) can sliced water chestnuts, drained

1 cup shredded roast chicken

1 cup frozen shelled edamame, thawed

¼ cup chopped cilantro

⅓ cup seasoned rice-wine vinegar

2 tablespoons reduced-sodium soy sauce

1 teaspoon sesame oil

1 teaspoon garlic powder

½ teaspoon ground ginger

1. Toss the coleslaw mix, scallions, water chestnuts, chicken, edamame, and cilantro together in a large bowl.

2. Whisk the vinegar, soy sauce, oil, garlic powder, and ginger together in a small bowl. Pour over the coleslaw mixture and toss to combine. Serve immediately, or refrigerate and serve chilled.

PER SERVING (2 CUPS): *190 Cal, 5 g Fat, 1 g Sat Fat, 0 g Trans Fat, 22 mg Chol, 772 mg Sod, 22 g Carb, 7 g Fib, 14 g Prot, 92 mg Calc.*

Tuna and Shells Salad

SERVES 6 | **PREP** 15 minutes | **COOK** 20 minutes

½ pound medium shell pasta

1 cup plain low-fat yogurt

2 tablespoons low-fat mayonnaise

¼ cup snipped dill

½ teaspoon salt

2 (6-ounce) cans light tuna in water, drained

4 celery stalks, sliced

4 scallions, sliced

1 cup frozen peas, thawed

1. Cook the pasta according to the package directions, omitting the salt if desired. Drain the pasta in a colander and rinse under cold running water until cool.

2. Stir the yogurt, mayonnaise, dill, and salt together in a large bowl. Add the pasta, tuna, celery, scallions, and peas and stir to combine.

PER SERVING (1¼ CUPS): *253 Cal, 3 g Fat, 1 g Sat Fat, 0 g Trans Fat, 22 mg Chol, 510 mg Sod, 36 g Carb, 3 g Fib, 20 g Prot, 113 mg Calc.*

Kids can...

Snip the dill with kids' safety scissors—it's great to keep a clean pair of these scissors in the kitchen for cutting herbs, scallions, and leafy greens.

Honey-Mustard Turkey Strips *toddler friendly* ☺

SERVES 4 | **PREP** 10 minutes | **BAKE** 20 minutes

¼ cup Dijon or yellow mustard

2 tablespoons honey

1½ teaspoons reduced-sodium soy sauce

¾ cup plain dried bread crumbs

1 pound boneless skinless turkey breast, cut into strips

1. Preheat the oven to 400°F. Spray a baking sheet with nonstick spray.

2. Whisk the mustard, honey, and soy sauce together in a small bowl. Place the bread crumbs on a plate. Dip the turkey strips into the honey-mustard mixture, then into the bread crumbs. Place on the baking sheet. Spray the turkey strips lightly with nonstick spray and bake, turning once, until cooked through, about 20 minutes.

PER SERVING (ABOUT 4 PIECES): *169 Cal, 2 g Fat, 0 g Sat Fat, 0 g Trans Fat, 50 mg Chol, 451 mg Sod, 17 g Carb, 1 g Fib, 20 g Prot, 52 mg Calc.*

Try it

Most commercially prepared chicken nuggets are full of added fat, whether you get them at the drive-thru or from the freezer section of your supermarket. This recipe makes nuggets with almost no added fat and uses turkey breast, which is generally moister and more flavorful than chicken breast. Mix a little extra honey-mustard for dipping if you like and serve it along with the strips.

Honey-Mustard Turkey Strips and Peas
and Prosciutto, page 203

Hummus Heads

SERVES 2 | PREP 10 minutes | NO COOK

2 romaine lettuce leaves, cut into very thin strips

¼ cup drained bottled roasted red pepper strips

8 cherry tomatoes, halved

4 pitted black olives, sliced

1 Kirby cucumber, sliced

2 whole-wheat English muffins, split in half and toasted

½ cup hummus

Place the lettuce, red pepper strips, tomatoes, olives, and cucumber slices in piles on a plate. Spread the English muffins with the hummus, then use the vegetables to make funny faces on them: lettuce or pepper strips can be hair, tomatoes or olives can be eyes, cucumber slices can be ears—use your imagination, adding any vegetables you like, and have fun!

PER SERVING (2 DECORATED ENGLISH MUFFIN HALVES): *279 Cal, 9 g Fat, 1 g Sat Fat, 0 g Trans Fat, 0 mg Chol, 819 mg Sod, 42 g Carb, 10 g Fib, 12 g Prot, 218 mg Calc.*

Kids can...

In addition to decorating their own sandwiches, kids can use plastic knives to halve the cherry tomatoes and slice the black olives.

Stoplight Pita Sandwiches

toddler friendly

1 cup farmer cheese

½ red bell pepper, diced

½ yellow bell pepper, diced

¼ cup shredded reduced-fat cheddar cheese

2 scallions, trimmed and sliced

⅛ teaspoon black pepper

3 mini whole-wheat pita breads, halved

Stir the farmer cheese, bell peppers, cheddar, scallions, and black pepper together in a medium bowl. Divide the mixture among the pita halves.

PER SERVING (2 PITA HALVES): *251 Cal, 10 g Fat, 6 g Sat Fat, 0 g Trans Fat, 33 mg Chol, 551 mg Sod, 19 g Carb, 3 g Fib, 19 g Prot, 81 mg Calc.*

Try it

Children love miniature foods, partly because small edibles are the right size for little hands and mouths, but also because anything scaled-down seems to appeal to their innate sense of humor. Make that appeal work for you; in addition to using mini pitas, try other healthful minis such as cherry tomatoes, baby zucchini, baby corn, Seckel pears, and baby bananas.

Lunch Wrap Spirals

SERVES 2 | **PREP** 10 minutes | **NO COOK**

2 large (8-inch) flour tortillas

2 tablespoons whipped cream cheese

4 chives or basil leaves, chopped

½ small avocado, peeled, pitted, and thinly sliced

6 spinach leaves, washed and dried

2 whole roasted red bell peppers, drained and cut into strips

Spread each tortilla with 1 tablespoon of the cream cheese and sprinkle with the chives. Layer the avocado slices, spinach leaves, and bell peppers evenly over each tortilla. Roll each up tightly. Cut each roll into 5 or 6 pieces with a serrated knife and lay the pieces on their sides so you can see the colorful spiral design.

PER SERVING (1 ROLL): *258 Cal, 12 g Fat, 4 g Sat Fat, 0 g Trans Fat, 11 mg Chol, 315 mg Sod, 33 g Carb, 5 g Fib, 7 g Prot, 101 mg Calc.*

Kids can...

Layer the avocado, spinach, and peppers over the cream cheese, then roll the tortillas up as snugly as possible.

Curried Sweet Potato Soup

SERVES 6 | **PREP** 15 minutes | **COOK** 30 minutes

2 teaspoons unsalted butter

1 onion, finely chopped

1 celery stalk, finely chopped

2 garlic cloves, minced

2 teaspoons curry powder

3 sweet potatoes (about 1½ pounds total), peeled and cut into 1-inch pieces

1 (32-ounce) box reduced-sodium chicken or vegetable broth

¾ teaspoon salt

8 ounces silken tofu

¼ teaspoon ground nutmeg

1. Melt the butter in a large, heavy saucepan over medium heat. Add the onion and cook until it begins to soften, about 3 minutes. Add the celery and cook until softened, about 2 minutes. Add the garlic and curry powder and cook until fragrant, about 30 seconds.

2. Add the sweet potatoes, broth, and salt and bring to a boil. Reduce the heat and simmer, uncovered, until the potatoes are tender, about 20 minutes.

3. Pulse the tofu in a food processor until smooth. Using a slotted spoon, scoop the potatoes out of the soup and add them to the food processor. Process until very smooth. Scrape the potato-tofu mixture back into the saucepan and whisk until the soup is smooth. Whisk in the nutmeg. If the mixture seems too thick, whisk in ½–1 cup water or broth. Reheat if necessary.

PER SERVING (1 CUP): 140 Cal, 4 g Fat, 2 g Sat Fat, 0 g Trans Fat, 6 mg Chol, 381 mg Sod, 22 g Carb, 3 g Fib, 6 g Prot, 56 mg Calc.

Smart move

Garnish the soup with a little low-fat plain yogurt, chopped celery, and nutmeg, if you like.

Black Bean Soup with Rice

SERVES 4 | PREP 10 minutes | COOK 20 minutes

2 teaspoons canola oil

1 onion, chopped

1 celery stalk, chopped

1 green bell pepper, chopped

1 tomato, chopped

2 garlic cloves, finely chopped

2 teaspoons chili powder

1½ teaspoons ground cumin

2 (15-ounce) cans black beans, rinsed and drained

1 (14½-ounce) can reduced-sodium chicken broth or vegetable broth

¼ cup chopped cilantro

2 cups cooked brown rice

1. Heat the oil over medium heat in a large saucepan. Add the onion and cook, stirring occasionally, until softened, about 4 minutes. Add the celery, pepper, tomato, and garlic and cook until the celery is softened, about 3 minutes. Add the chili powder and cumin and cook 1 minute longer.

2. Add the beans to the saucepan and mash coarsely with a potato masher or large fork. Pour in the broth; increase the heat to high and bring the soup to a boil. Reduce the heat to medium and simmer until the flavors are blended, about 10 minutes. Stir in the cilantro. Serve each bowl of soup topped with a mound of brown rice.

PER SERVING (1½ CUPS SOUP AND ½ CUP RICE): *296 Cal, 5 g Fat, 0 g Sat Fat, 0 g Trans Fat, 0 mg Chol, 568 mg Sod, 50 g Carb, 12 g Fib, 13 g Prot, 84 mg Calc.*

Try it

Looking for something even quicker than quick-cooking brown rice? Many supermarkets now sell shelf-stable pouches of fully cooked brown rice or multigrain pilaf. Just heat in the microwave for a minute or two and they're ready.

Hey, Kids! Check It Out!

Cook Up Some Fun

The following recipes are designed specifically with young cooks in mind. These super-fun dishes require little or no chopping or stove time, so most kids and preteens can accomplish them with just a bit of help and supervision from adults. And they're great to share with your friends and family!

Breakfast Berry Sundaes (page 111)
Layers of creamy yogurt and fresh fruit make for a colorful start to the day.

Pineapple Crush Smoothies (page 123)
Get an adult to help with the blender and this cool treat is ready in minutes.

Chinese Chicken Salad (page 128)
Tangy and refreshing! A great lunch or light dinner.

Tuna and Shells Salad (page 129)
Have an adult boil the pasta and you can put this salad together in minutes.

Hummus Heads (page 133)
Fun and healthful open-face sandwiches that will bring out the artist in everyone.

Teriyaki Tempeh Kabobs (page 181)
Make these yummy kabobs ahead of time and get an adult to help with broiling them at the last minute.

Personal Pizzas (page 195)
Everyone gets involved designing their own pizzas. Great for a party!

Watermelon Cake with Raspberry Sauce (page 211)
Have an adult slice the watermelon, then get creative decorating this fruit-based centerpiece.

Pomegranate Granita (page 215)
An icy treat that's fun to watch freeze.

Better Than Take-Out

What's so great about making take-out classics like cheese steaks and tacos at home? Lots! Not only is it fun, but also home-cooked meals are generally more healthful than what you can get at fast-food restaurants. Best of all, you can get really creative with the ingredients you use and customize everything to your family's tastes. Here are some of our favorite recipes you can help Mom or Dad prepare at home:

Quick Quesadillas (page 127)
Ready in minutes! Makes a super after-school snack.

Greens Pizza (page 141)
Starting with a prebaked crust makes this pie a cinch to put together.

Philly Cheese Steaks (page 148)
An all-time classic, perfect for lunch or dinner.

Beef and Black Bean Burgers (page 151)
Add your favorite toppings: ketchup, mustard, pickles, coleslaw, you name it!

Ham and Turkey Stromboli (page 153)
A pizza-parlor favorite that's great for parties.

Fish Tacos with Mango Salsa (page 175)
Crunchy, tangy, and super-easy to make.

Sushi Shrimp Rolls (page 180)
Making the rolls is just as much fun as eating them.

Vegetable Fried Rice (page 183)
Packed with tasty vegetarian ingredients.

Oven-Baked Sweet Potato Fries (page 199)
Tons more flavor than regular fries.

Greens Pizza

SERVES 8 | PREP 20 minutes | COOK/BAKE 30 minutes

2 (1-pound) bunches Swiss chard, well rinsed

1 tablespoon extra-virgin olive oil

2 onions, halved and sliced

3 garlic cloves, minced

¼ teaspoon salt

1 large tomato, chopped

1 tablespoon balsamic vinegar

⅛ teaspoon black pepper

1½ cups grated reduced-fat Monterey Jack cheese

1 (8-ounce) prebaked whole-wheat pizza crust

1. Pull the leaves away from the stems and tough middle ribs of the chard. (Discard the stems and ribs, or slice and add to soups or stews.) Chop the leaves coarsely. Heat the oil in a large pot or Dutch oven over medium heat. Add the onions and cook, stirring occasionally, until tender, about 5 minutes. Add the garlic and cook until fragrant, about 30 seconds.

2. Preheat the oven to 400°F. Place a baking sheet in the oven to heat.

3. Add the chard and salt to the onions in the pot, cover, and let cook 3–4 minutes. Stir in the tomato and cook, uncovered, stirring occasionally, until the tomato is very soft, 5–7 minutes. Stir in the vinegar and pepper.

4. Sprinkle ½ cup of the cheese over the crust. Spoon the chard mixture over the cheese, then sprinkle with the remaining 1 cup cheese. Carefully place the pizza on the preheated baking sheet and bake until the cheese melts, about 15 minutes. Cool 5 minutes before cutting into 8 slices.

PER SERVING (1 SLICE): *189 Cal, 8 g Fat, 4 g Sat Fat, 0 g Trans Fat, 15 mg Chol, 580 mg Sod, 23 g Carb, 6 g Fib, 11 g Prot, 249 mg Calc.*

Try it

Tall, dark, and . . . leafy! Greens such as chard, kale, collards, and spinach contain a mother lode of nutrients and antioxidants, but they're not everyone's favorite served straight up. This recipe takes advantage of the universal appeal of pizza to introduce the delicious taste of chard. To work more dark, leafy greens into your meals, try slicing them very thinly and letting them cook into soups, stews, and rice dishes.

Grilled Cheese Triangles

SERVES 1 | **PREP** 5 minutes | **COOK** 5 minutes

2 (1-ounce) slices reduced-fat cheddar cheese

2 slices multigrain bread

½ McIntosh apple, peeled, cored, and thinly sliced

1. Place a slice of cheese on one slice of the bread. Spread the apple slices evenly over the cheese. Top with the remaining cheese and bread.

2. Spray a small nonstick skillet with nonstick spray and place over medium heat. Place the sandwich in the skillet and cook until the bottom is golden brown, about 2 minutes. Carefully flip the sandwich and cook until the other side is browned, about 2 minutes longer. Cut into triangles and serve.

PER SERVING (1 SANDWICH): *285 Cal, 6 g Fat, 2 g Sat Fat, 0 g Trans Fat, 14 mg Chol, 847 mg Sod, 39 g Carb, 5 g Fib, 19 g Prot, 455 mg Calc.*

Try it

Introducing new foods in tandem with old favorites is often a good tactic. We've added crisp, sweet apple to this sandwich to help newbies adjust to the assertive (but delicious!) flavor and texture of whole-grain bread.

FAMILY DINNERS

Island Ginger Beef Stew

SERVES 8 | PREP 30 minutes | COOK 2 hours 20 minutes

2 pounds boneless bottom round steak, trimmed and cut into 1-inch chunks

1 teaspoon salt

½ teaspoon black pepper

2 medium onions, chopped

4 garlic cloves, minced

1 (1-inch) piece ginger, peeled and grated on the small holes of a box grater

2 tablespoons all-purpose flour

1 (14½-ounce) can reduced-sodium beef broth

1 (14½-ounce) can diced tomatoes

2 bay leaves

¼ teaspoon ground allspice

5 large carrots, sliced

3 celery ribs, sliced

1 (14-ounce) can corn, drained

½ jicama, peeled and diced

1. Sprinkle the beef with the salt and pepper. Spray a large, heavy pot with nonstick spray and set over medium-high heat. In two batches, add the beef and cook, turning occasionally, until browned, about 6 minutes. Transfer the beef to a bowl. Add the onions to the pot. Cook, stirring occasionally, until softened, about 5 minutes.

2. Reduce the heat to medium and add the garlic and ginger; cook until fragrant, about 30 seconds. Stir in the flour and cook until lightly browned, 1–2 minutes. Stir in the broth, tomatoes, bay leaves, and allspice. Add the beef back to the pot. Cover the pot, adjust the heat, and simmer 1½ hours.

3. Add the carrots, celery, and corn to the pot and cook until the vegetables are tender, about 30 minutes. Stir in the jicama. Remove from the heat and discard the bay leaves.

PER SERVING (1½ CUPS): *256 Cal, 6 g Fat, 2 g Sat Fat, 0 g Trans Fat, 69 mg Chol, 762 mg Sod, 25 g Carb, 5 g Fib, 26 g Prot, 68 mg Calc.*

Tangy Slow-Cooker Pulled Brisket

SERVES 12 | PREP 15 minutes | COOK 4 to 5 hours on High or 8 to 10 hours on Low

1 (3-pound) first-cut or flat-cut brisket, trimmed

2 large Spanish onions, halved and sliced

4 garlic cloves, minced

2 teaspoons chili powder

1 teaspoon ground cumin

1 (28-ounce) can diced tomatoes

¼ cup packed dark brown sugar

¼ cup red-wine vinegar

2 tablespoons reduced-sodium soy sauce

1. Spray a large nonstick skillet with nonstick spray and set over medium-high heat. Add the brisket and cook, turning once, until browned, about 6 minutes. Transfer the brisket to a 5- or 6-quart slow cooker.

2. Add the onions to the skillet and cook, stirring frequently, until the onions are softened, about 5 minutes. Add the garlic, chili powder, and cumin and cook 1 minute longer. Scrape the onions on top of the brisket. Combine the tomatoes, brown sugar, vinegar, and soy sauce in a medium bowl and pour over the brisket.

3. Cover and cook until the brisket is fork-tender, 4–5 hours on High or 8–10 hours on Low. Transfer the brisket to a plate and cool 15 minutes. With two forks, shred the brisket. Return the meat to the cooker and toss with the sauce.

PER SERVING (1 CUP SHREDDED BEEF AND SAUCE): *235 Cal, 9 g Fat, 3 g Sat Fat, 1 g Trans Fat, 67 mg Chol, 312 mg Sod, 14 g Carb, 2 g Fib, 23 g Prot, 44 mg Calc.*

Try it

This makes a good amount of delicious brisket, so consider cooking once and planning two meals from it: Serve it one night piled onto crusty whole-wheat rolls with Creamy Coleslaw with Apple and Red Onion (see page 201) on the side; and another night over a mound of Gold and White Mashed Potatoes (see page 198) with a steamed veggie on the side.

Hey, Moms! Check It Out!

The following recipes are designed to appeal to your family's taste buds and help you out when you're juggling a crazy schedule or simply need a little flexibility.

Slow-Cooker Solutions Nothing beats the deep, rich flavor of slowly simmered soups and stews. By doing your prep work when you have a few moments, either the night before or early in the morning, then leaving the rest to your slow cooker, you can have these soulful, satisfying meals on the table even on busy weeknights:

Tangy Slow-Cooker Pulled Brisket (page 146)

Slow-Cooker Pork Loin with Apricot Glaze (page 154)

Slow-Cooker Greek Chicken Stew (page 164)

Slow-Cooker Paella with Chicken Sausage (page 165)

Slow-Cooker Chickpea and Barley Soup (page 196)

No-Cook Recipes Even your stove needs a cool day off once in a while. Here are some recipes you and your family can enjoy without heating up the kitchen:

Breakfast Berry Sundaes (page 111)

Pineapple Crush Smoothies (page 123)

Chinese Chicken Salad (page 128)

Hummus Heads (page 133)

Stoplight Pita Sandwiches (page 134)

Lunch Wrap Spirals (page 135)

Turkey Tabbouleh (page 167)

Creamy Coleslaw with Apple and Red Onion (page 201)

Watermelon Cake with Raspberry Sauce (page 211)

Frozen Fruit Pops (page 214)

Pomegranate Granita (page 215)

Big Batch Bounty Cooking up a hefty batch of a family favorite and freezing the leftovers for another meal is a tried-and-true way to plan ahead for busy days. Soups and stews will generally keep refrigerated for 3 or 4 days, frozen for up to 3 months. Here are our top suggestions for cooking once and eating twice:

Island Ginger Beef Stew (page 144)

Middle Eastern Lamb and Eggplant (page 158)

Mexican Chicken Chili (page 160)

Moroccan Turkey Tagine (page 166)

Shrimp and Sausage Jambalaya (page 178)

Mushroom Lasagna (page 187)

Dinner in 20 Minutes or Less Quick, healthful recipes can be a lifesaver on busy weeknights. Recruit a helper to set the table and your family can be sitting down to one of these delicious dinners in no time.

Beef and Black Bean Burgers (page 151)

Confetti Orzo with Ham and Vegetables (page 155)

Turkey Tabbouleh (page 167)

Sweet-and-Spicy Salmon with Broccoli Slaw (page 176)

Basque-Style Cod with Crunchy Panko (page 177)

Shrimp with Cherry Tomatoes and Feta (page 179)

Vegetable Fried Rice (page 183)

Philly Cheese Steaks

SERVES 4 | PREP 15 minutes | COOK 15 minutes

1 teaspoon safflower or canola oil

2 large onions, thinly sliced

2 Italian frying peppers, sliced

2 garlic cloves, finely chopped

¼ teaspoon salt

¾ pound boneless sirloin steak, trimmed and thinly sliced

4 (¾-ounce) slices reduced-fat provolone cheese

1 dill pickle, sliced

4 small (2-ounce) crusty whole-wheat rolls, split lengthwise

1. Heat the oil in a nonstick skillet over medium-high heat. Add the onions, peppers, and garlic and sprinkle with ⅛ teaspoon of the salt. Cook, stirring occasionally, until the onions are browned, about 10 minutes. Transfer to a small bowl and set aside.

2. Wipe out the skillet and spray with nonstick spray. Place over medium-high heat. Sprinkle the steak with the remaining ⅛ teaspoon salt and place half of it in the skillet. Cook until browned on both sides, about 2 minutes; transfer to a plate. Repeat with the remaining steak.

3. Place a slice of cheese and a few pickle slices on each roll. Divide the beef and onion mixture among the rolls and serve at once.

PER SERVING (1 FILLED ROLL): *352 Cal, 12 g Fat, 4 g Sat Fat, 0 g Trans Fat, 59 mg Chol, 755 mg Sod, 37 g Carb, 6 g Fib, 29 g Prot, 348 mg Calc.*

Kids can...

Place the cheese and pickle slices on the rolls.

Creamy Coleslaw with Apple and Red Onion, page 201, and Philly Cheese Steaks

Cuban Picadillo

1 large onion, finely chopped

4 garlic cloves, finely chopped

1 bay leaf

1 pound ground lean beef (7% fat or less)

¼ teaspoon salt

1 (14½-ounce) can diced tomatoes with juice

½ (4-ounce) can tomato paste

⅓ cup sliced pitted green olives

⅓ cup raisins

2 teaspoons dried oregano

2 teaspoons ground cumin

8 Boston or butter lettuce leaves

1. Spray a large nonstick skillet with nonstick spray and set over medium-high heat. Add the onion, garlic, and bay leaf and cook, stirring occasionally, until the onion is softened, about 4 minutes.

2. Add the beef and salt; cook, breaking the meat up with a wooden spoon, until browned, about 3 minutes. Tilt the skillet and spoon off any excess fat. Stir in the tomatoes, tomato paste, olives, raisins, oregano, and cumin. Simmer over medium-low heat, stirring occasionally, until the flavors have blended, about 8 minutes.

3. Remove and discard the bay leaf. Spoon the mixture into the lettuce leaves.

PER SERVING (1¼ CUPS PICADILLO AND 2 LETTUCE LEAVES): *264 Cal, 7 g Fat, 2 g Sat Fat, 1 g Trans Fat, 62 mg Chol, 650 mg Sod, 24 g Carb, 3 g Fib, 27 g Prot, 103 mg Calc.*

Try it

For a heartier meal, serve this savory dish wrapped in tortillas.

Beef and Black Bean Burgers

SERVES 6 | PREP 10 minutes | BROIL 10 minutes

1 (14-ounce) can black beans, rinsed and drained

¾ pound ground lean beef (7% fat or less)

¼ cup mild salsa

¼ cup chopped parsley

¼ teaspoon salt

6 whole-wheat hamburger buns

1. Preheat the broiler; spray the broiler pan with nonstick spray.

2. Place the beans in a large bowl and mash them coarsely with a potato masher or large fork; some of the beans should remain whole for texture. Add the beef, salsa, parsley, and salt and mix with a spoon or your hands until blended.

3. Shape the mixture into 6 patties and place the patties on the broiler pan. Broil, turning once, until cooked through and browned, about 10 minutes. Serve on the buns.

PER SERVING (1 SANDWICH): *239 Cal, 6 g Fat, 2 g Sat Fat, 0 g Trans Fat, 38 mg Chol, 497 mg Sod, 29 g Carb, 6 g Fib, 19 g Prot, 66 mg Calc.*

Kids can...

Mash the beans with a potato masher, then help shape the burger mixture into patties.

Ham and Turkey Stromboli

SERVES 6 | PREP 20 minutes | BAKE 30 minutes

1 pound frozen whole-wheat pizza dough, thawed

2 tablespoons honey mustard

¼ pound thinly sliced low-sodium baked Virginia ham

¼ pound thinly sliced low-sodium honey-baked turkey breast

¼ pound thinly sliced reduced-fat Jarlsberg cheese

½ cup drained bottled roasted red peppers, rinsed and chopped

12 arugula leaves

1. Preheat the oven to 400°F. Spray a baking sheet with nonstick spray.

2. On a lightly floured surface, roll or pat one-sixth of the dough out into a circle about 6 inches in diameter. Spread with 1 teaspoon of the honey mustard and top with one-sixth of the ham, turkey, cheese, roasted peppers, and arugula. Roll the dough up into a thin cylinder, encasing the filling; tuck the ends under and pinch the edges with your fingers to seal. Repeat with the remaining ingredients, making a total of 6 rolls.

3. Arrange the rolls, seam side down, on the baking sheet. Spray the tops with nonstick spray. Bake until golden, about 30 minutes. Let the rolls cool 3–4 minutes, then use a serrated knife to slice them in half.

PER SERVING (1 STROMBOLI): *305 Cal, 8 g Fat, 3 g Sat Fat, 0 g Trans Fat, 29 mg Chol, 375 mg Sod, 39 g Carb, 4 g Fib, 18 g Prot, 238 mg Calc.*

Smart move

When preparing foods with your kids, think about using the time to talk in a fun, positive way about healthy food choices. Ask them why they think food prepared at home might be better than what they could get at a take-out restaurant. You might mention that by cooking at home, you can add more great vegetables and healthful whole grains. Plus you don't have to rely on flavor from excess salt, fat, and sugar when you start with good fresh ingredients.

Slow-Cooker Pork Loin with Apricot Glaze

SERVES 10 | PREP 20 minutes | COOK 4 to 5 hours on High or 8 to 10 hours on Low

1 (2½-pound) boneless pork loin, trimmed

1 teaspoon salt

¼ teaspoon black pepper

2 teaspoons extra-virgin olive oil

6 carrots, sliced on the diagonal

4 parsnips, peeled and sliced on the diagonal

1 large onion, chopped

4 garlic cloves, minced

1 cup apricot preserves

1 tablespoon Dijon mustard

1. Sprinkle the pork with the salt and pepper. Heat the oil in a large nonstick skillet over medium-high heat. Add the pork and cook, turning frequently, until browned on all sides, about 10 minutes.

2. Transfer the pork to a 5- or 6-quart slow cooker. Arrange the carrots and parsnips around the pork. Add the onion and garlic to the skillet. Cook, stirring frequently, until the garlic begins to brown, about 4 minutes. Remove from the heat; stir in the preserves and mustard. Pour the mixture over the pork.

3. Cover and cook until the pork is fork-tender, 4–5 hours on High or 8–10 hours on Low. Transfer the pork to a cutting board; cut into 10 slices. Serve with the vegetables and sauce.

PER SERVING (1 SLICE PORK WITH 1 CUP VEGETABLES AND SAUCE): *332 Cal, 9 g Fat, 3 g Sat Fat, 0 g Trans Fat, 64 mg Chol, 360 mg Sod, 40 g Carb, 4 g Fib, 25 g Prot, 63 mg Calc.*

Kids can...

After the carrots and parsnips have been sliced, kids can arrange them around the pork in the slow cooker.

Confetti Orzo with Ham and Vegetables

SERVES 4 | PREP 5 minutes | COOK 15 minutes

1 red bell pepper, chopped

3 cups reduced-sodium chicken broth

1 (16-ounce) bag frozen mixed vegetables, thawed

½ teaspoon dried thyme

¼ teaspoon salt

1 cup tricolor orzo

6 ounces low-sodium baked Virginia ham, diced

3 tablespoons finely grated Parmesan cheese

2 scallions, trimmed and sliced

1. Spray a large nonstick skillet with nonstick spray and set over medium-high heat. Add the pepper and cook, stirring occasionally, until softened, about 3 minutes. Add the broth, mixed vegetables, thyme, and salt and bring to a boil; add the orzo. Bring back to a boil, cover the skillet, and cook, stirring occasionally, until the orzo is tender, about 10 minutes.

2. Stir in the ham, cheese, and scallions and cook until heated through.

PER SERVING (1¼ CUPS): 311 Cal, 4 g Fat, 1 g Sat Fat, 0 g Trans Fat, 22 mg Chol, 1,097 mg Sod, 52 g Carb, 7 g Fib, 21 g Prot, 113 mg Calc.

Kids can...

Rinse the bell pepper and scallions and pat them dry with paper towels or a clean kitchen towel.

Minestrone with Pancetta

SERVES 8 | PREP 20 minutes | COOK 30 minutes

1 tablespoon extra-virgin olive oil

3 carrots, sliced

2 onions, chopped

2 celery stalks, sliced

3 ounces thinly sliced pancetta, chopped

4 garlic cloves, finely chopped

1 large russet potato, peeled and diced

1 (15-ounce) can cannellini beans, rinsed and drained

6 cups reduced-sodium beef or vegetable broth

2 small zucchini, diced

1 (14½-ounce) can diced tomatoes

⅛ teaspoon salt

8 teaspoons shredded Parmesan cheese

1. Heat the oil in a large, heavy saucepan over medium heat. Add the carrots, onions, celery, pancetta, and garlic. Cook until the vegetables are softened, about 10 minutes. Add the potato and cook 2 minutes longer.

2. Meanwhile, blend half of the beans with 1 cup of the broth in a food processor or blender until almost smooth. Add the pureed bean mixture, zucchini, tomatoes, salt, and remaining 5 cups broth to the pan. Cook over medium-low heat until the potato is tender, about 15 minutes.

3. Stir in the whole beans and simmer until heated through, about 2 minutes. Ladle into bowls and sprinkle each with cheese.

PER SERVING (1¼ CUPS SOUP AND 1 TEASPOON SHREDDED PARMESAN): *196 Cal, 7 g Fat, 2 g Sat Fat, 0 g Trans Fat, 9 mg Chol, 439 mg Sod, 24 g Carb, 5 g Fib, 10 g Prot, 80 mg Calc.*

Kids can...

Older kids can open the cans of beans and tomatoes with a can opener; younger ones can pour the beans into a colander set in the sink, then run cold water over the beans until they're thoroughly rinsed.

Middle Eastern Lamb and Eggplant

SERVES 8 | PREP 20 minutes | COOK 1 hour

2 pounds boneless leg of lamb, trimmed and cut into 1-inch chunks

½ teaspoon salt

2 onions, chopped

1 tablespoon extra-virgin olive oil

1 eggplant, diced

4 garlic cloves, finely chopped

1 teaspoon cinnamon

¼ teaspoon black pepper

1 (28-ounce) can diced tomatoes with juice

1. Spray a large nonstick skillet with nonstick spray and set over medium-high heat. Sprinkle the lamb with ¼ teaspoon of the salt. Add half the lamb to the skillet and cook, stirring frequently, until browned, about 5 minutes. Transfer the lamb to a bowl and repeat with the remaining lamb. Set aside.

2. Cook the onions in the same skillet over medium heat, stirring occasionally, until softened, about 5 minutes. Push the onions to one side of the skillet and add the oil. When the oil becomes hot, add the eggplant, garlic, and remaining ¼ teaspoon salt and cook until the eggplant is softened, about 8 minutes. Add the cinnamon and pepper and cook 1 minute. Add the tomatoes and browned lamb to the skillet and simmer, uncovered, until the lamb is tender, about 30 minutes.

PER SERVING (1 CUP): *207 Cal, 8 g Fat, 2 g Sat Fat, 1 g Trans Fat, 65 mg Chol, 324 mg Sod, 12 g Carb, 4 g Fib, 23 g Prot, 40 mg Calc.*

Try it

Serve the lamb and eggplant on a platter with a ring of Israeli couscous or whole-wheat couscous around it.

Chicken in Coconut Curry Sauce

SERVES 4 | PREP 10 minutes | COOK 20 minutes

2 teaspoons extra-virgin olive oil

1 onion, diced

2 teaspoons curry powder

1 cup light (reduced-fat) coconut milk

1 (14½-ounce) can diced tomatoes

2 tablespoons tomato paste

1 pound skinless, boneless chicken breast, cut into 1-inch cubes

¼ teaspoon salt

1 (5-ounce) bag baby spinach leaves

1 cup frozen peas

1. Heat the oil in a large nonstick skillet over medium heat. Add the onion and cook, stirring occasionally, until softened, about 4 minutes. Add the curry powder and cook, stirring, until fragrant, about 1 minute. Stir in the coconut milk, tomatoes, and tomato paste and bring to a boil. Reduce the heat and cook, stirring occasionally, until the sauce thickens slightly, 6–8 minutes.

2. Add the chicken and salt to the skillet and cook until the chicken is no longer pink in the center, about 4 minutes. Add the spinach and peas and cook until the spinach is wilted and the peas are tender, about 3 minutes.

PER SERVING (1½ CUPS): *272 Cal, 9 g Fat, 4 g Sat Fat, 0 g Trans Fat, 63 mg Chol, 440 mg Sod, 21 g Carb, 7 g Fib, 28 g Prot, 75 mg Calc.*

Smart move

Everyone likes to feel that their tastes and preferences are important, so let your kids help create a weekly shopping list that includes some of their favorite fruits, veggies, and whole-grain foods. Involving them in healthful choices may make them less likely to request junk foods.

Mexican Chicken Chili

SERVES 10 | PREP 30 minutes | COOK 1 hour 45 minutes

6 bone-in skinless chicken breast halves

2 tablespoons canola oil

3 onions, chopped

6 garlic cloves, minced

¼ cup chili powder

3 tablespoons ground cumin

2 tablespoons packed light brown sugar

2 tablespoons unsweetened cocoa powder

1 tablespoon dried oregano

2 teaspoons ground coriander

1 (28-ounce) can crushed tomatoes in puree

1 (12-ounce) bottle beer or 1½ cups chicken broth

1 teaspoon salt

2 (15-ounce) cans kidney beans, rinsed and drained

1. Combine the chicken and enough water to cover in a large, heavy pot and bring to a boil over high heat. Reduce the heat, cover the pot, and simmer gently until the chicken is cooked through, about 12 minutes. Drain the chicken, reserving the cooking liquid. Cool the chicken, remove and discard the bones, and coarsely shred the meat.

2. Meanwhile, place the same pot over medium-high heat and add the oil. Add the onions and cook, stirring occasionally, until browned, about 10 minutes. Add the garlic and cook 1 minute. Stir in the chili powder, cumin, brown sugar, cocoa powder, oregano, and coriander and cook until the spices are fragrant, about 1 minute. Add the tomatoes, beer, salt, and 3½ cups of the reserved cooking liquid. Bring to a simmer; reduce the heat to medium low, cover, and cook, stirring occasionally, 1 hour.

3. Add the beans. Simmer, uncovered, until the chili thickens, about 30 minutes. Add the shredded chicken and simmer until heated through.

PER SERVING (1½ CUPS): *239 Cal, 6 g Fat, 1 g Sat Fat, 0 g Trans Fat, 44 mg Chol, 488 mg Sod, 26 g Carb, 8 g Fib, 22 g Prot, 103 mg Calc.*

Braised Bok Choy and Chicken with Soba Noodles

SERVES 4 | PREP 15 minutes | COOK 10 minutes

1 (8-ounce) package soba noodles

1 pound skinless, boneless chicken breast, thinly sliced

¼ teaspoon salt

4 scallions, sliced

1 tablespoon grated peeled fresh ginger

2 garlic cloves, minced

2 tablespoons hoisin sauce

8 heads baby bok choy, quartered

2 teaspoons sesame oil

1. Cook the noodles according to the package directions; drain, reserving ½ cup of the cooking liquid.

2. Meanwhile, spray a large nonstick skillet with nonstick spray and set over medium-high heat. Sprinkle the chicken with the salt; add it to the skillet and cook, stirring frequently, until it starts to brown slightly, about 3 minutes. Add the scallions, ginger, and garlic and cook, stirring occasionally, for 1 minute. Stir in the hoisin sauce. Add the bok choy and the reserved cooking liquid. Cover the skillet and cook until the bok choy is tender, 4–5 minutes.

3. Add the noodles and oil to the skillet and toss until combined.

PER SERVING (2 CUPS): *243 Cal, 6 g Fat, 1 g Sat Fat, 0 g Trans Fat, 63 mg Chol, 422 mg Sod, 20 g Carb, 4 g Fib, 29 g Prot, 183 mg Calc.*

Try it

Delicious, tender soba noodles are made with whole-wheat and buckwheat flours. You can substitute whole-wheat linguine if you like.

Slow-Cooker Greek Chicken Stew

SERVES 6 | PREP 30 minutes | COOK 4½ to 5½ hours on High or 8½ to 10½ hours on Low

6 skinless, boneless chicken thighs (about 1½ pounds)

½ teaspoon salt

¼ teaspoon black pepper

6 medium Red Bliss potatoes, sliced

8 garlic cloves, minced

2 leeks, cleaned and chopped (white and light-green parts only)

1 fennel bulb, halved and sliced

1 teaspoon dried oregano

1 (14½-ounce) can diced tomatoes

1 (10-ounce) bag frozen artichoke hearts, partially thawed

1. Sprinkle the chicken with ¼ teaspoon of the salt and ⅛ teaspoon of the pepper. Spray a large nonstick skillet with nonstick spray and set over medium-high heat. Add the chicken and cook, turning once, until browned, 8–10 minutes.

2. Transfer the chicken to a 5- or 6-quart slow cooker. Arrange the potatoes, garlic, leeks, and fennel around the chicken and sprinkle with the oregano and remaining ¼ teaspoon salt and ⅛ teaspoon pepper. Pour in the tomatoes.

3. Cover and cook 4–5 hours on High or 8–10 hours on Low. Add the artichokes and cook until thawed, about 30 minutes longer.

PER SERVING (1 CHICKEN THIGH AND 1 CUP SAUCE AND VEGETABLES): *374 Cal, 9 g Fat, 2 g Sat Fat, 0 g Trans Fat, 76 mg Chol, 387 mg Sod, 47 g Carb, 7 g Fib, 28 g Prot, 74 mg Calc.*

Kids can...

Arrange the cut vegetables in the slow cooker, then measure out and sprinkle in the oregano and salt and pepper.

Slow-Cooker Paella with Chicken Sausage

SERVES 6 | PREP 15 minutes | COOK 1 to 2 hours on High or 3 to 4 hours on Low

1 tablespoon extra-virgin olive oil

1 large onion, chopped

1 green bell pepper, chopped

1 red or yellow bell pepper, chopped

1 zucchini, halved and sliced

1 (8-ounce) package sliced mushrooms

3 garlic cloves, minced

1 (8-ounce) package yellow rice mix

1 (14½-ounce) can diced tomatoes

2 cups water

12 ounces fully-cooked reduced-fat chicken sausage, sliced

1. Heat the oil in a large skillet over medium heat. Add the onion and cook, stirring frequently, until the onion is softened, about 5 minutes. Add the peppers, zucchini, mushrooms, and garlic and cook until the vegetables soften, about 3 minutes. Transfer the vegetables to a 5- or 6-quart slow cooker. Add the rice mix, tomatoes, and water.

2. Cook the sausage in the same skillet over medium-high heat until browned, about 2 minutes; add the sausage to the slow cooker. Cover and cook until the rice is just tender and the liquid is absorbed, 1–2 hours on High or 3–4 hours on Low.

PER SERVING (1½ CUPS): *269 Cal, 7 g Fat, 1 g Sat Fat, 0 g Trans Fat, 44 mg Chol, 1,055 mg Sod, 40 g Carb, 4 g Fib, 14 g Prot, 39 mg Calc.*

Smart move

If you've got teens at home who'd like to take charge of dinner once or twice a week, slow-cooker recipes can be a good option: Slow-cooking is relatively safe, and if cooked on High, most recipes will be ready by dinner time if started after school.

Moroccan Turkey Tagine

SERVES 8 | PREP 25 minutes | COOK 50 minutes

1 tablespoon extra-virgin olive oil

1 large red onion, chopped

1¼ pounds skinless, boneless turkey breast, cut into 1-inch chunks

¼ teaspoon salt

1 teaspoon ground cumin

1 teaspoon ground turmeric

½ teaspoon cinnamon

1 butternut squash, peeled, halved, seeded, and cut into 1-inch chunks

1 Granny Smith apple, peeled, cored, and diced

1 large tomato, diced

1 (19-ounce) can chickpeas, rinsed and drained

1 (14½-ounce) can reduced-sodium chicken broth

4 dried figs, chopped

¼ cup chopped cilantro

1. Heat the oil in a large, heavy saucepan over medium-high heat. Add the onion and cook, stirring frequently, until softened, about 5 minutes. Push the onion to one side of the pan and add the turkey. Sprinkle with the salt and cook, stirring frequently, until the turkey is browned on all sides, about 5 minutes. Add the cumin, turmeric, and cinnamon; cook, stirring, until fragrant, about 30 seconds.

2. Add the squash, apple, tomato, chickpeas, broth, and figs and bring to a boil. Reduce the heat and simmer, covered, until the turkey and vegetables are tender, about 35 minutes. Remove from the heat and sprinkle with the cilantro.

PER SERVING (1 CUP): 223 Cal, 3 g Fat, 1 g Sat Fat, 0 g Trans Fat, 59 mg Chol, 340 mg Sod, 24 g Carb, 6 g Fib, 26 g Prot, 68 mg Calc.

Smart move

Purchasing precut veggies in your supermarket's produce section can be a great time-saver. If you can find butternut squash already prepared and diced, you might want to invest in it—you'll need about 4 cups to equal 1 whole squash.

Turkey Tabbouleh

SERVES 4 | PREP 20 minutes | NO COOK

1 cup bulgur wheat

1½ cups boiling water

1 bunch scallions, trimmed and sliced

1 bunch mint, chopped

1 bunch flat-leaf parsley, chopped

1 English (seedless) cucumber, peeled and diced

1 pint grape tomatoes, halved

½ pound cooked turkey breast, diced

¼ cup lemon juice

1 tablespoon extra-virgin olive oil

½ teaspoon salt

¼ teaspoon black pepper

1. Place the bulgur in a large bowl and pour the boiling water over it. Cover the bowl with plastic wrap and allow the bulgur to stand at room temperature until the grains are tender and the liquid is absorbed, about 15 minutes.

2. Add the scallions, mint, parsley, cucumber, tomatoes, and turkey. Stir the lemon juice, oil, salt, and pepper together in a small bowl. Drizzle over the bulgur mixture and toss to combine.

PER SERVING (1¾ CUPS): *276 Cal, 5 g Fat, 1 g Sat Fat, 0 g Trans Fat, 47 mg Chol, 352 mg Sod, 37 g Carb, 11 g Fib, 24 g Prot, 109 mg Calc.*

Kids can...

Stir the lemon juice, oil, salt, and pepper together with a fork and drizzle this dressing over the bulgur mixture.

Turkey and Rice "Mice"

toddler friendly

SERVES 8 | PREP 10 minutes | BAKE 45 minutes

2 slices whole-wheat bread

1 pound ground skinless turkey breast

1 cup cooked brown rice

1 small onion, grated

¼ cup ketchup

¼ teaspoon salt

½ cup unsweetened apple juice

4 sliced pitted black olives

Carrot slices and strips

1. Preheat the oven to 350°F.

2. Place the bread in a food processor and pulse to make fine crumbs. Transfer the crumbs to a large bowl and add the turkey, rice, onion, ketchup, and salt. Mix with your hands or a spoon until well blended. Form the mixture into 8 small oval loaves and place the loaves in a 9 × 13-inch baking pan. Pour the apple juice into the pan. Bake until the mice are cooked through, about 45 minutes.

3. Remove the mice from the pan with a spatula. Press 2 olive slices into each for eyes and make ears and tails with carrot slices and strips.

PER SERVING (1 "MOUSE"): 142 Cal, 1 g Fat, 0 g Sat Fat, 0 g Trans Fat, 47 mg Chol, 248 mg Sod, 13 g Carb, 1 g Fib, 19 g Prot, 18 mg Calc.

Try it

Cuteness counts! Have a conversation with your kids about these critters, let them stick on the eyes, ears, and tails, and see if they have an attitude adjustment toward brown rice and turkey.

Turkey and Rice "Mice" and Creamed Spinach, page 202

Garden Meatloaf

SERVES 6 | PREP 20 minutes | COOK/BAKE 1 hour 15 minutes

2 teaspoons extra-virgin olive oil

1 medium onion, chopped

3 carrots, shredded

1 medium zucchini, shredded

1 red bell pepper, finely chopped

1 celery stalk, finely chopped

¼ pound (about 8) cremini mushrooms, chopped

3 garlic cloves, finely chopped

1¼ pounds ground skinless turkey breast

¾ cup old-fashioned rolled oats

½ cup unsweetened applesauce

¼ cup chopped parsley

1 large egg, beaten

1 teaspoon salt

1. Preheat the oven to 350°F. Line a 9 × 13-inch baking pan with foil. Heat the oil in a large nonstick skillet over medium heat. Add the onion and cook until softened, about 5 minutes. Add the carrots, zucchini, pepper, and celery and cook until softened, about 5 minutes. Add the mushrooms and garlic and cook until the mushrooms are softened, about 3 minutes.

2. Combine the turkey, oats, applesauce, parsley, egg, and salt in a large bowl. Gently fold in the vegetables. Scrape the mixture into the pan and use your hands to shape it into a loaf. Bake until browned and an instant-read thermometer inserted into the center of the meatloaf registers 165°F, about 1 hour. Let stand 10 minutes before cutting into 6 slices.

PER SERVING (1 SLICE): *216 Cal, 4 g Fat, 1 g Sat Fat, 0 g Trans Fat, 97 mg Chol, 470 mg Sod, 19 g Carb, 4 g Fib, 27 g Prot, 53 mg Calc.*

Smart move

Make your box grater an ally in healthy eating! Add shredded vegetables such as carrots and zucchini to meat dishes, sauces, and baked goods. In addition to flavor, you'll be adding vitamins, fiber, and antioxidants.

Mini Fishwiches

SERVES 4 | PREP 20 minutes | COOK 10 minutes

1 (¾-pound) cod fillet

¼ cup all-purpose flour

½ cup buttermilk

¾ cup whole-wheat cracker crumbs

1 tablespoon finely chopped parsley

½ teaspoon salt

¼ teaspoon garlic powder

2 teaspoons extra-virgin olive oil

4 mini whole-wheat buns

1. Cut the fish into 4 equal pieces. Place the flour in a shallow bowl and the buttermilk in another. Stir the crumbs, parsley, salt, and garlic powder together in a third bowl. Coat each piece of fish first with the flour, then with the buttermilk, and finally with the crumb mixture.

2. Heat the oil in a medium nonstick skillet over medium-high heat. Add the fish and cook, turning once, until browned and just opaque in the center, about 8 minutes. Place each piece in a bun.

PER SERVING (1 SANDWICH): *277 Cal, 8 g Fat, 1 g Sat Fat, 0 g Trans Fat, 34 mg Chol, 621 mg Sod, 34 g Carb, 4 g Fib, 19 g Prot, 85 mg Calc.*

Try it

Even very young children will enjoy personalizing a sandwich with spreads and toppings, and it's a way for them to begin to experiment with new tastes and textures. Set out a plate of healthful and flavorful extras like lettuce, tomato slices, red onion rings, sliced olives, capers, pickles, tartar sauce, and ketchup to go with these sandwiches, and let the whole family get in on the fun.

Mini Fishwiches and Oven-Baked Sweet Potato Fries, page 199

Fish Tacos with Mango Salsa

SERVES 4 | PREP 15 minutes | COOK 10 minutes

½ teaspoon ground cumin

¼ teaspoon chipotle chile powder or regular chili powder

¼ teaspoon salt

1 pound flaky white fish fillet such as tilapia or halibut

1 cup plain low-fat yogurt

3 tablespoons chopped cilantro

2 tablespoons lime juice

1 tablespoon reduced-fat mayonnaise

1½ cups shredded cabbage

8 (6-inch) corn tortillas

½ cup mango salsa

1. Combine the cumin, chile powder, and salt in a small bowl. Sprinkle the mixture evenly over the fish. Coat a large nonstick skillet with nonstick spray and set over medium-high heat. Add the fish and cook until opaque in the center, about 3 minutes per side. Set the fish aside to cool for a few minutes, then flake it into pieces with a fork.

2. Meanwhile, stir the yogurt, cilantro, lime juice, and mayonnaise together in a medium bowl. Add the cabbage and toss to combine.

3. Warm the tortillas in the microwave according to the package directions. Divide the fish and cabbage evenly among the tortillas. Serve with the salsa on the side.

PER SERVING (2 TACOS AND 2 TABLESPOONS SALSA): *296 Cal, 6 g Fat, 1 g Sat Fat, 0 g Trans Fat, 40 mg Chol, 507 mg Sod, 33 g Carb, 4 g Fib, 30 g Prot, 269 mg Calc.*

Try it

Mango salsa is sold in the refrigerator section of most supermarkets, or you can make your own by combining 1 peeled and pitted diced mango, 1 diced tomato, ¼ cup diced red onion, ½ cup peeled and seeded diced cucumber, ¼ cup chopped cilantro, and salt and pepper to taste. Mangoes are a delicious source of vitamins A, C, and E, as well as other antioxidants, so it's great to get them on the table.

Sweet-and-Spicy Salmon with Broccoli Slaw

SERVES 4 | PREP 10 minutes | BROIL 10 minutes

2 tablespoons packed light brown sugar

1 teaspoon five-spice powder

¼ teaspoon salt

4 (¼-pound) pieces skinless salmon fillet

2 tablespoons reduced-sodium soy sauce

2 tablespoons rice vinegar

2 teaspoons sesame oil

1 (12-ounce) package broccoli slaw

¼ cup chopped cilantro

3 scallions, trimmed and sliced

1. Stir the brown sugar, five-spice powder, and salt together in a small bowl. Sprinkle the mixture over the tops of the salmon fillets.

2. Preheat the broiler. Spray the broiler pan with nonstick spray and place it about 6 inches from the heat until very hot. Carefully place the salmon fillets on the hot broiler pan and broil until browned on the outside and almost cooked in the center, about 7 minutes. Remove the pan from the oven and let the salmon continue to cook on the hot pan until cooked all the way through, about 5 minutes.

3. Meanwhile, whisk the soy sauce, vinegar, and oil together in a large bowl. Add the broccoli slaw, cilantro, and scallions and toss. Serve alongside the salmon.

PER SERVING (1 SALMON FILLET AND 1 CUP SLAW): *224 Cal, 7 g Fat, 1 g Sat Fat, 0 g Trans Fat, 65 mg Chol, 561 mg Sod, 13 g Carb, 4 g Fib, 27 g Prot, 77 mg Calc.*

Smart move

Eating oily fish such as salmon and trout is a surefire way to improve your family's diet. What to do if you have kids who complain about fishy-tasting fish? First of all, always buy the best-quality seafood you can and try to use it the same day you purchase it; fresh fish should smell like the sea. Second, don't overcook it, and serve it with strong but complementary flavors—try citrus, soy sauce, or brown sugar for salmon; sage or capers for trout. And, of course, a lemon wedge never hurts!

Basque-Style Cod with Crunchy Panko

SERVES 4 | PREP 10 minutes | BAKE 10 minutes

1 zucchini, cut into ribbons with a vegetable peeler

1 tomato, sliced

1 yellow bell pepper, thinly sliced

5 kalamata olives, pitted and chopped

4 (¼-pound) pieces skinless cod fillet

4 teaspoons Dijon mustard

¼ cup panko bread crumbs

2 teaspoons melted butter

½ lemon, seeds removed

Preheat the oven to 450°F. Arrange the zucchini, tomato, pepper, and olives in an 8-inch-square baking dish. Place the cod on top and spread each fillet with 1 teaspoon mustard. Press 1 tablespoon bread crumbs on top of each piece of fish and drizzle the bread crumbs with the melted butter. Squeeze the lemon over the dish. Bake until the vegetables are tender and the fish is opaque in the center, about 10 minutes.

PER SERVING (1 PIECE FISH AND ⅔ CUP VEGETABLES): *155 Cal, 5 g Fat, 2 g Sat Fat, 0 g Trans Fat, 48 mg Chol, 275 mg Sod, 9 g Carb, 2 g Fib, 20 g Prot, 33 mg Calc.*

Kids can...

Use a butter knife to spread the mustard over the fillets, then press the bread crumbs onto each.

Shrimp and Sausage Jambalaya

SERVES 10 | PREP 20 minutes | COOK 35 minutes

1 tablespoon extra-virgin olive oil

4 bell peppers, any color, diced

2 onions, diced

1 pound reduced-fat turkey kielbasa, thinly sliced

4 garlic cloves, finely chopped

2 teaspoons paprika

1½ teaspoons dried oregano

1 teaspoon salt

¼ teaspoon cayenne, or more to taste

5 cups water

1 (28-ounce) can diced tomatoes

2 cups long-grain white rice

2 tablespoons tomato paste

1½ pounds medium shrimp, peeled and deveined

1. Heat the oil in a large, heavy pot over medium-high heat. Add the peppers, onions, and kielbasa and cook, stirring occasionally, until the vegetables soften, about 8 minutes. Add the garlic, paprika, oregano, salt, and cayenne and cook, stirring, 1 minute.

2. Stir in the water, tomatoes, rice, and tomato paste and bring to a boil. Reduce the heat to medium low and cook, covered, until the rice is tender and most of the liquid has been absorbed, about 20 minutes.

3. Add the shrimp and cook, covered, until cooked through, about 5 minutes.

PER SERVING (1½ CUPS): *308 Cal, 4 g Fat, 1 g Sat Fat, 0 g Trans Fat, 117 mg Chol, 837 mg Sod, 46 g Carb, 3 g Fib, 21 g Prot, 78 mg Calc.*

Try it

Jambalaya will keep in the refrigerator for about 3 days or frozen for several months. When reheating it, take care not to stir it too much or the rice grains will get mushy.

Shrimp with Cherry Tomatoes and Feta

SERVES 4 | PREP 10 minutes | COOK 10 minutes

⅔ cup whole-wheat couscous

2 teaspoons extra-virgin olive oil

¾ pound medium shrimp, peeled and deveined

¼ teaspoon salt

2 garlic cloves, finely chopped

1 pint cherry tomatoes, halved

1 teaspoon dried oregano

¼ cup reduced-sodium chicken broth

¼ cup chopped dill

3 tablespoons crumbled feta cheese

1. Prepare couscous according to package directions, omitting the salt if desired.

2. Meanwhile, heat the oil in a large skillet over medium-high heat. Add the shrimp and salt and cook, stirring, until the shrimp begin to turn pink, 1–2 minutes.

3. Add the garlic, tomatoes, and oregano and cook until the tomatoes soften, about 1 minute. Add the broth and cook until most of the liquid has evaporated, 1–2 minutes. Stir in the dill and feta cheese and cook 1 minute longer. Serve over the couscous.

PER SERVING (1 CUP SHRIMP MIXTURE AND ½ CUP COUSCOUS): *263 Cal, 5 g Fat, 2 g Sat Fat, 0 g Trans Fat, 132 mg Chol, 415 mg Sod, 35 g Carb, 6 g Fib, 21 g Prot, 87 mg Calc.*

Kids can...

Help peel the shrimp and crumble the feta with their fingers or a fork.

Sushi Shrimp Rolls

SERVES 4 | PREP 25 minutes | COOK 20 minutes

1½ cups sushi rice

1½ cups water

1½ tablespoons seasoned rice vinegar

1 avocado, peeled, pitted, and thinly sliced

½ lemon, seeds removed

4 sheets nori

1 small cucumber, peeled, seeded, and cut into matchstick pieces

12 peeled, cooked medium shrimp, chopped

Soy sauce, wasabi, and pickled ginger for serving (optional)

1. Combine the rice and water in a medium saucepan and bring to a boil over high heat. Reduce the heat, cover, and simmer until the water is absorbed, about 18 minutes. Remove from the heat and let stand, covered, 10 minutes. Transfer the rice to a large glass bowl; sprinkle with the vinegar and toss to combine. Cool to room temperature.

2. Place the avocado on a small plate and squeeze the lemon juice over it to prevent browning. Lay a nori sheet on a clean countertop, or on a sushi rolling mat if you have one. Wet your fingers with water and spread ¾ cup of the cooled rice evenly onto the nori. Place one-fourth of the avocado slices, cucumber, and shrimp in the center of the sheet. Keeping the filling in place with your fingers and starting from the long side, roll into a tight cylinder, rolling up the mat if using one. Repeat with the remaining ingredients, making 4 rolls.

3. Slice each roll into 8 pieces with a serrated knife. Serve with the soy sauce, wasabi, and pickled ginger, if using.

PER SERVING (1 ROLL): *295 Cal, 7 g Fat, 1 g Sat Fat, 0 g Trans Fat, 27 mg Chol, 140 mg Sod, 50 g Carb, 6 g Fib, 9 g Prot, 19 mg Calc.*

Try it

Making sushi rolls at home is a favorite family cooking activity. Once you try it, you may find the kids asking to do it weekly and creating original rolls using their favorite ingredients. Nori, sushi rice, wasabi, and pickled ginger are available at most grocery stores these days; you can buy extras like sushi rolling mats, dipping bowls, and authentic chopsticks at specialty stores if your family really gets into it.

Teriyaki Tempeh Kabobs

SERVES 4 | PREP 10 minutes | BAKE 15 minutes

1 (8-ounce) package tempeh, cut into 12 squares

12 cherry tomatoes

12 small white mushrooms

¼ cup teriyaki sauce

1. Preheat the oven to 350°F. Coat a 9 × 13-inch baking pan with nonstick spray.

2. Have ready 4 long bamboo or metal skewers. Thread a piece of tempeh on a skewer, followed by a tomato and a mushroom. Repeat again so you have 3 pieces of each food on the skewer. Place it in the pan and repeat with the remaining skewers.

3. Brush each skewer all over with 1 tablespoon teriyaki sauce. Bake until the vegetables are tender, about 15 minutes.

PER SERVING (1 SKEWER): *143 Cal, 6 g Fat, 1 g Sat Fat, 0 g Trans Fat, 0 mg Chol, 701 mg Sod, 12 g Carb, 4 g Fib, 13 g Prot, 72 mg Calc.*

Smart move

What fruits and veggies are in season in your area right now? A family outing to your local farmers' market or farm stand is a fun way to find out. Although this recipe uses vegetables that are usually fresh and tasty year-round, consider adding chunks of a seasonal local hero, such as zucchini, bell peppers, cauliflower, onions, or even cooked potato.

Vegetable Fried Rice

SERVES 6 | PREP 10 minutes | COOK 10 minutes

1 teaspoon canola oil

4 scallions, trimmed and sliced

2 garlic cloves, finely chopped

1 tablespoon grated peeled fresh ginger

¼ pound snow peas, sliced lengthwise

1 red bell pepper, chopped

2 cups cooked white rice

2 cups cooked brown rice

1 (10-ounce) package frozen mixed vegetables, thawed

8 ounces firm tofu, diced

2 large eggs, beaten

3 tablespoons reduced-sodium soy sauce

2 teaspoons sesame oil

1. Heat the canola oil in a large skillet over medium-high heat. Add the scallions, garlic, and ginger and cook, stirring, until fragrant, about 30 seconds. Add the snow peas and pepper and cook until the pepper softens, about 1 minute. Add the white and brown rice, mixed vegetables, and tofu and cook, stirring, until heated through, about 5 minutes.

2. Push the rice mixture to the edge of the skillet, making a hollow in the center. Pour in the eggs and cook, stirring, until the eggs are cooked. Stir the eggs into the rice, drizzle with the soy sauce and sesame oil, and toss to combine.

PER SERVING (1¼ CUPS): 293 Cal, 8 g Fat, 2 g Sat Fat, 0 g Trans Fat, 71 mg Chol, 358 mg Sod, 42 g Carb, 5 g Fib, 14 g Prot, 307 mg Calc.

Smart move

This recipe mixes brown rice with white rice—a good way to introduce brown rice to kids (and adults) who might have reservations about it on its own. Packets of shelf-stable, already cooked rice are the quickest way to get this dish on the table, or you can stop by your local Chinese restaurant and pick up a pint container each of white and brown rice.

Fusilli with Broccoli, Beans, and Walnuts

SERVES 4 | PREP 10 minutes | COOK 20 minutes

2 cups whole-wheat fusilli pasta

1 head broccoli, florets halved and stems peeled and thinly sliced

2 teaspoons extra-virgin olive oil

6 garlic cloves, thinly sliced

1 (15-ounce) can cannellini beans, rinsed and drained

Pinch red pepper flakes

¼ cup grated Parmesan cheese

⅓ cup chopped walnuts

1. Cook the fusilli according to the package directions, omitting the salt if desired. Four minutes before it's done, add the broccoli to the boiling water and cook until the pasta and broccoli are tender. Drain, reserving ½ cup of the cooking water.

2. Return the pot to medium heat. Add the oil and garlic and cook until the garlic begins to turn golden, about 2 minutes. Stir in the beans and pepper flakes. Add the reserved pasta water, then the drained pasta and broccoli. Add the cheese and walnuts and toss until combined.

PER SERVING (2 CUPS): *307 Cal, 11 g Fat, 2 g Sat Fat, 0 g Trans Fat, 4 mg Chol, 253 mg Sod, 44 g Carb, 10 g Fib, 13 g Prot, 142 mg Calc.*

Smart move

Whole-wheat pasta is a boon for those trying to work more whole grains into the family diet. But remember that whole wheat's nuttier flavor and firmer texture can take some getting used to, even for adults. If your family needs a little help surmounting the "brown barrier," here are a few tricks: Don't start with spaghetti; whole-grain pasta's firmer texture may seem more palatable in shapes like fusilli or elbows. Consider beginning with a mix of half whole-wheat, half regular pasta in your recipes. Finally, you could try one of the "hybrid" pastas that blend white flour with other grains and extra fiber.

Mushroom Lasagna

SERVES 12 | PREP 30 minutes | COOK/BAKE 50 minutes

1 large onion, finely chopped

1 pound cremini mushrooms, sliced

4 garlic cloves, finely chopped

¾ teaspoon salt

2 (10-ounce) packages frozen chopped spinach, thawed and squeezed dry

1 tablespoon unsalted butter

¼ cup all-purpose flour

4 cups low-fat (1%) milk

¾ cup grated Parmesan cheese

1 (15-ounce) container part-skim ricotta cheese

2 cups shredded fat-free mozzarella cheese

12 basil leaves, chopped

1 (8-ounce) box no-cook lasagna noodles

1. Preheat the oven to 350°F. Spray a 9 × 13-inch baking dish with nonstick spray. Spray a large nonstick skillet with nonstick spray and set it over medium-high heat. Add the onion and cook until softened, about 3 minutes. Add the mushrooms, garlic, and ¼ teaspoon of the salt and cook, stirring, until the mushrooms are tender, about 5 minutes. Stir in the spinach and heat through.

2. Melt the butter in a large saucepan over medium heat. Stir in the flour and cook, stirring, 1 minute. Increase heat to medium high and whisk in 1 cup of milk. Cook until the mixture begins to thicken. Whisk in remaining 3 cups milk. Cook, stirring frequently, until mixture simmers and thickens, about 8 minutes. Stir in ½ cup of the Parmesan and the remaining ½ teaspoon salt; remove from the heat.

3. Stir the ricotta, mozzarella, and basil together in a bowl. Fold in ¼ cup of the white sauce. Spoon one-third of the white sauce into the baking dish. Layer in half the mushroom-spinach mixture, half the noodles, and half the ricotta mixture. Repeat layers once. Pour remaining sauce over the top and sprinkle with the remaining ¼ cup Parmesan. Bake until sauce is bubbling and noodles are tender, about 30 minutes. Cool 10 minutes, then cut into 12 (3-inch) squares.

PER SERVING (1 SQUARE): *257 Cal, 9 g Fat, 6 g Sat Fat, 0 g Trans Fat, 28 mg Chol, 465 mg Sod, 27 g Carb, 3 g Fib, 19 g Prot, 455 mg Calc.*

Indian-Spiced Lentils

SERVES 6 | PREP 10 minutes | COOK 45 minutes

1 cup brown basmati rice

2 teaspoons canola oil

1 onion, chopped

4 garlic cloves, finely chopped

1 tablespoon minced peeled fresh ginger

1 teaspoon ground cumin

1 teaspoon ground turmeric

2 tomatoes, chopped

2 cups chopped cauliflower florets

2½ cups water

1 cup dried red lentils

¾ teaspoon salt

1 lemon or lime, halved

Chopped cilantro

1. Prepare the rice according to the package directions, omitting the salt if desired.

2. Meanwhile, heat the oil in a large saucepan over medium-high heat. Add the onion, garlic, and ginger and cook, stirring occasionally, until the onion softens, about 2 minutes. Stir in the cumin and turmeric and cook 1 more minute. Add the tomatoes and cauliflower and cook 2 minutes. Add the water and lentils and bring to a boil. Reduce the heat to medium low and simmer, covered, until the lentils are tender, about 35 minutes.

3. Stir in the salt. Squeeze the lemon over the lentils, garnish with the cilantro, and serve with the rice.

PER SERVING (1 CUP LENTILS AND VEGETABLES AND ½ CUP RICE): *255 Cal, 3 g Fat, 0 g Sat Fat, 0 g Trans Fat, 0 mg Chol, 314 mg Sod, 49 g Carb, 8 g Fib, 11 g Prot, 50 mg Calc.*

Kids can...

Squeeze the lemon juice over the lentils and garnish the dish with cilantro.

Spaghetti Pie

SERVES 6 | PREP 15 minutes | BAKE 30 minutes

4 cups cooked spaghetti (about ½ pound uncooked)

1 (10-ounce) package frozen chopped broccoli, thawed and squeezed dry

1 cup shredded smoked mozzarella cheese

½ cup part-skim ricotta cheese

¼ cup finely grated Parmesan cheese

1 large egg, beaten

1 teaspoon Italian seasoning

1½ cups marinara sauce, warmed in the microwave

Chopped parsley leaves

1. Preheat the oven to 350°F. Coat a 9-inch springform pan with nonstick spray.

2. Stir the spaghetti, broccoli, mozzarella, ricotta, Parmesan, egg, and Italian seasoning together in a large bowl. Scrape the mixture into the springform pan and level the top.

3. Bake until the top is golden brown, about 30 minutes. Cool in the pan about 5 minutes. Protecting your hands with oven mitts, remove the side of the pan. Cut the pie into 6 wedges and serve topped with the marinara and parsley.

PER SERVING (1 WEDGE AND ¼ CUP MARINARA SAUCE): *291 Cal, 10 g Fat, 5 g Sat Fat, 1 g Trans Fat, 59 mg Chol, 395 mg Sod, 36 g Carb, 4 g Fib, 15 g Prot, 264 mg Calc.*

Kids can...

Stir the spaghetti mixture together and scrape it into the prepared pan.

Crumb-Topped Mac ☺ 'n' Cheese

SERVES 8 | PREP 15 minutes | COOK/BAKE 55 minutes

12 ounces (about 3 cups) whole-wheat elbow macaroni

2 teaspoons unsalted butter

1 small onion, finely chopped

2 tablespoons all-purpose flour

1 teaspoon dried thyme

1 (14½-ounce) can reduced-sodium chicken broth

1 (12-ounce) package frozen butternut squash puree, thawed

1 cup fat-free half-and-half

1½ cups shredded reduced-fat sharp cheddar cheese

¼ teaspoon pumpkin pie spice

¼ teaspoon salt

¼ cup plus 2 tablespoons grated Parmesan cheese

2 slices whole-wheat bread, torn into pieces

1. Preheat the oven to 350°F. Spray a 9 × 13-inch baking pan with nonstick spray.

2. Cook macaroni according to package directions, omitting the salt if desired.

3. Meanwhile, melt the butter in a large saucepan over medium heat. Add the onion and cook, stirring occasionally, until softened, about 5 minutes. Whisk in the flour and thyme and cook until the flour starts to brown, about 1 minute. Whisk in the broth and squash puree. Whisk in the half-and-half and bring the sauce to a simmer. Stir in the cheddar, pumpkin pie spice, salt, and ¼ cup of the Parmesan.

4. Drain the pasta and combine with the sauce. Pour the mixture into the pan and level the top. Pulse the bread in a food processor to make bread crumbs. Combine the bread crumbs with the remaining 2 tablespoons Parmesan and sprinkle the mixture over the casserole. Bake until the macaroni is hot and bubbling and the topping is crisp, about 30 minutes.

PER SERVING (1 CUP): *315 Cal, 8 g Fat, 5 g Sat Fat, 0 g Trans Fat, 21 mg Chol, 525 mg Sod, 47 g Carb, 5 g Fib, 16 g Prot, 281 mg Calc.*

Sesame Noodles with Green Vegetables

SERVES 4 | **PREP** 10 minutes | **COOK** 15 minutes

6 ounces whole-wheat linguine

Florets from 2 broccoli crowns

½ pound sugar snap peas

½ pound frozen shelled edamame

3 scallions, trimmed and sliced

2 tablespoons reduced-sodium soy sauce

1 tablespoon sesame oil

½ garlic clove, minced

1. Cook the linguine according to the package directions, omitting the salt if desired. Four minutes before it's done, add the broccoli, snap peas, and edamame to the boiling water and cook until the pasta and vegetables are tender. Drain, reserving ½ cup of the cooking water.

2. Combine the pasta, vegetables, and scallions in a large bowl. Whisk the soy sauce, oil, garlic, and reserved pasta water together in a small bowl and pour it over the pasta and vegetables. Toss to coat.

PER SERVING (1¾ CUPS): *311 Cal, 7 g Fat, 1 g Sat Fat, 0 g Trans Fat, 0 mg Chol, 356 mg Sod, 47 g Carb, 12 g Fib, 16 g Prot, 123 mg Calc.*

Kids can...

Mix the soy sauce, oil, garlic, and pasta water together with a fork and pour it over the pasta and vegetables.

Personal Pizzas

SERVES 6 | PREP 25 minutes | BAKE 15 minutes

1½ pounds pizza dough, thawed if frozen

1½ teaspoons extra-virgin olive oil

1½ cups pizza sauce

2 cups shredded fat-free mozzarella cheese

1 bell pepper, any color, sliced

12 pitted black olives

6 slices zucchini, halved

3 grape or cherry tomatoes, halved

Any other toppings you like

1. On a lightly floured surface, cut the dough into 6 equal pieces and roll each into a smooth ball. Cover the balls with plastic wrap and let rest on the counter for 10 minutes.

2. Preheat the oven to 450°F. Spray two large baking sheets with nonstick spray. Pat or roll each ball into a circle about 7 inches in diameter and place them on the baking sheets. Brush the edges of each with the oil. Spread the sauce evenly over the dough and sprinkle each with ⅓ cup of the cheese. Decorate each pizza as desired with the vegetables.

3. Bake until the crusts are golden brown and the cheese is bubbling, about 15 minutes. Cool the pizzas on the pan about 5 minutes before slicing.

PER SERVING (1 PIZZA TOPPED WITH VEGETABLES): *399 Cal, 3 g Fat, 0 g Sat Fat, 0 g Trans Fat, 4 mg Chol, 1,135 mg Sod, 61 g Carb, 4 g Fib, 22 g Prot, 563 mg Calc.*

Try it

You'll find ready-made pizza dough in the freezer case of most supermarkets, and some markets even carry whole-wheat dough. You can also ask at your local pizza parlor and they'll usually give you a ball for a buck or two, with the added benefit that you don't have to wait for it to thaw. And if you're really ambitious, you can find a pizza dough recipe online, start from scratch, and make it a fun afternoon project.

Slow-Cooker Chickpea and Barley Soup

SERVES 6 | PREP 15 minutes | COOK 4 to 5 hours on High or 8 to 10 hours on Low

2 teaspoons extra-virgin olive oil

1 medium onion, chopped

3 garlic cloves, minced

1 (19-ounce) can chickpeas, rinsed and drained

½ cup pearl barley

3 carrots, finely chopped

1 sweet potato, peeled and diced

¼ cup chopped parsley

1 teaspoon ground cumin

2 (32-ounce) boxes reduced-sodium fat-free chicken broth

1 (5-ounce) bag baby spinach

1 tablespoon balsamic vinegar

1. Heat the oil in a large nonstick skillet over medium heat. Add the onion and cook, stirring frequently, until lightly browned, about 5 minutes. Add the garlic and cook until fragrant, about 30 seconds.

2. Scrape the onion mixture into a 5- or 6-quart slow cooker. Add the chickpeas, barley, carrots, sweet potato, parsley, and cumin. Pour the broth over the chickpeas and vegetables. Cover and cook until the vegetables are fork-tender, 4–5 hours on High or 8–10 hours on Low. Stir in the spinach and vinegar and cook 5 minutes longer.

PER SERVING (1⅔ CUPS): *230 Cal, 3 g Fat, 0 g Sat Fat, 0 g Trans Fat, 0 mg Chol, 971 mg Sod, 43 g Carb, 8 g Fib, 10 g Prot, 69 mg Calc.*

Try it

Browning the onion and garlic before adding them to the cooker sweetens and intensifies their flavor. But if you're pressed for time, by all means skip this extra step; your soup will be plenty flavorful and delicious even if you add them raw.

SAVVY SIDES

Gold and White Mashed Potatoes

SERVES 6 | **PREP** 15 minutes | **COOK** 25 minutes

1¼ pounds Yukon Gold potatoes, peeled and cut into 1-inch chunks

5 garlic cloves, peeled

1 (15 ½-ounce) can cannellini beans, rinsed and drained

½ cup low-fat buttermilk

½ teaspoon salt

¼ teaspoon ground white pepper

1. Place the potatoes and garlic in a large pot with enough cold, salted water to cover by 3 inches and bring to a boil. Reduce the heat and simmer until fork-tender, 20–25 minutes; drain, reserving ½ cup of the cooking water.

2. Return the potatoes and garlic to the pot. Add the beans, buttermilk, salt, and pepper. Mash with a potato masher or large fork, adding the reserved cooking water a few tablespoons at a time, until the potatoes are smooth.

PER SERVING (½ CUP): *126 Cal, 0 g Fat, 0 g Sat Fat, 0 g Trans Fat, 1 mg Chol, 379 mg Sod, 25 g Carb, 3 g Fib, 5 g Prot, 43 mg Calc.*

Try it

White beans give this mash a boost of fiber and protein, and their mild flavor and light color help them blend in seamlessly. Consider adding mashed white beans to other creamy foods to improve their nutrition: dips, cheese sauces, thick soups, and baked pasta dishes.

Oven-Baked Sweet Potato Fries

SERVES 4 | PREP 10 minutes | BAKE 35 minutes

2 large sweet potatoes, scrubbed and skins left on

1½ teaspoons extra-virgin olive oil

½ teaspoon coarse sea salt or kosher salt

¼ teaspoon ground allspice

1. Preheat the oven to 400°F. Spray a nonstick baking pan with nonstick spray.

2. Quarter the potatoes lengthwise. Cut each quarter into 4 wedges; you should have 32 wedges in all. Toss the potatoes with the oil, salt, and allspice in a large bowl. Arrange in a single layer on the pan and bake until the potatoes are cooked through and crisp, about 35 minutes, turning them once halfway through baking.

PER SERVING (8 FRIES): *108 Cal, 2 g Fat, 0 g Sat Fat, 0 g Trans Fat, 0 mg Chol, 297 mg Sod, 22 g Carb, 3 g Fib, 2 g Prot, 26 mg Calc.*

Smart move

Getting your family to enjoy these delicious baked fries (and cutting back on the fried ones) is a great step toward a healthier diet. Sweet potatoes have even more beta-carotene than carrots, and leaving the potatoes unpeeled increases their fiber.

Grain and Orzo Pilaf

SERVES 6 | PREP 10 minutes | COOK 45 minutes

1½ teaspoons unsalted butter

1 small onion, chopped

2 garlic cloves, finely chopped

½ cup pearl barley

½ cup long-grain brown rice

3 cups reduced-sodium chicken broth

½ teaspoon dried thyme

¼ teaspoon salt

½ cup whole-wheat orzo

1 cup water

¼ cup chopped flat-leaf parsley

1. Melt the butter in a medium saucepan over medium heat. Add the onion and cook, stirring occasionally, until softened, about 5 minutes. Add the garlic, barley, and rice and cook, stirring, until the garlic is fragrant, about 1 minute. Add the broth, thyme, and salt and bring to a boil. Reduce the heat and simmer, covered, 20 minutes.

2. Add the orzo and water, cover again, and simmer until the liquid is absorbed and the grains are tender, 20 minutes longer. Add the parsley and fluff with a fork.

PER SERVING (¾ CUP): *187 Cal, 2 g Fat, 1 g Sat Fat, 0 g Trans Fat, 3 mg Chol, 413 mg Sod, 36 g Carb, 6 g Fib, 7 g Prot, 29 mg Calc.*

Try it

Here's a delicious alternative to white rice to put into your menu rotation. The brown rice and barley make this dish rich in B vitamins and a great source of fiber.

Creamy Coleslaw with Apple and Red Onion

SERVES 6 | PREP 15 minutes | NO COOK

½ cup plain low-fat yogurt

1 tablespoon reduced-fat sour cream

1 tablespoon white-wine vinegar

1½ teaspoons Dijon mustard

1 teaspoon sugar

½ teaspoon celery salt

½ small head green cabbage, finely sliced

1 large carrot, shredded

½ small red onion, thinly sliced

1 small McIntosh apple, peeled, cored, and shredded

Whisk the yogurt, sour cream, vinegar, mustard, sugar, and celery salt together in a large bowl. Add the cabbage, carrot, onion, and apple and toss until thoroughly combined. Cover and refrigerate for at least 15 minutes or up to 8 hours to allow the flavors to blend. Toss again just before serving.

PER SERVING (¾ CUP): *55 Cal, 1 g Fat, 0 g Sat Fat, 0 g Trans Fat, 2 mg Chol, 188 mg Sod, 11 g Carb, 2 g Fib, 2 g Prot, 76 mg Calc.*

Try it

Many children prefer vegetables in their raw, crunchy state over cooked ones, so think about serving more slaws, crudités, and salads of all kinds if they work better for your young eaters.

Creamed Spinach

SERVES 4 | PREP 10 minutes | COOK 10 minutes

2 shallots, chopped

2 garlic cloves, minced

1 (16-ounce) bag frozen chopped spinach, thawed and squeezed dry

⅓ cup part-skim ricotta cheese

2 tablespoons grated Parmesan cheese

⅛ teaspoon ground nutmeg

⅛ teaspoon salt

Spray a large skillet with nonstick spray and set it over medium heat. Add the shallots and cook, stirring occasionally, until softened, about 5 minutes. Stir in the garlic and spinach and cook until heated through, about 3 minutes. Stir in the ricotta, Parmesan, nutmeg, and salt and cook, stirring, until the mixture is heated through and blended, about 2 minutes.

PER SERVING (½ CUP): *76 Cal, 2 g Fat, 2 g Sat Fat, 0 g Trans Fat, 8 mg Chol, 227 mg Sod, 7 g Carb, 3 g Fib, 6 g Prot, 177 mg Calc.*

Try it

Spinach is an excellent source of folate and beta-carotene, and a good source of vitamin C, so it's worthwhile to serve it to your kids early and often.

Peas and Prosciutto

SERVES 4 | PREP 10 minutes | COOK 10 minutes

1½ teaspoons extra-virgin olive oil

3 shallots, sliced

2 garlic cloves, finely chopped

1 (16-ounce) bag frozen peas

2 ounces thinly sliced prosciutto, chopped

¼ cup thinly sliced basil leaves

⅛ teaspoon salt

⅛ teaspoon black pepper

Heat the oil in a large nonstick skillet over medium heat. Add the shallots and garlic and cook, stirring, until fragrant, about 1 minute. Add the peas and cook until heated through, about 5 minutes. Remove from the heat and stir in the prosciutto, basil, salt, and pepper.

PER SERVING (¾ CUP): *147 Cal, 4 g Fat, 1 g Sat Fat, 0 g Trans Fat, 13 mg Chol, 475 mg Sod, 19 g Carb, 6 g Fib, 10 g Prot, 38 mg Calc.*

Kids can...

Rinse the basil, then pat it dry with paper towels or a clean kitchen towel and pick the leaves from the stems.

Butternut Squash Puree 😊

SERVES 4 | PREP 5 minutes | COOK 10 minutes

2 (12-ounce) packages frozen butternut squash puree

⅓ cup apple juice

1 tablespoon maple syrup

1 teaspoon unsalted butter

1 teaspoon lemon juice

¼ teaspoon salt

Combine the squash and apple juice in a medium saucepan over medium heat. Cook, stirring occasionally and breaking up the frozen squash, until the mixture is heated through, about 10 minutes. Stir in the syrup, butter, lemon juice, and salt.

PER SERVING (¾ CUP): *128 Cal, 1 g Fat, 1 g Sat Fat, 0 g Trans Fat, 3 mg Chol, 150 mg Sod, 30 g Carb, 2 g Fib, 3 g Prot, 55 mg Calc.*

Smart move

Beta-carotene–rich vegetables such as sweet potatoes, carrots, and winter squash like butternut are a delicious part of a healthful diet. Introduce your kids to all these vegetables, and also consider adding purees of them to soups, pastas, and baked goods.

SWEET DESSERTS

Harvest Apple Squares

SERVES 24 | PREP 20 minutes | BAKE 50 minutes

1 cup all-purpose flour

1 cup old-fashioned rolled oats

1 cup plus 2 tablespoons whole-wheat pastry flour

½ cup sugar

6 tablespoons cold, unsalted butter, cut into chunks

½ cup apple juice

5 McIntosh or other firm apples, peeled, cored, and chopped

1 teaspoon cinnamon

1 teaspoon vanilla extract

¼ teaspoon ground nutmeg

1. Preheat the oven to 350°F. Spray a 9 × 13-inch baking pan with nonstick spray.

2. Place the all-purpose flour, oats, 1 cup of the whole-wheat flour, and ¼ cup of the sugar in a food processor and pulse until combined. Add the butter and pulse until blended. Add the apple juice and pulse until the dough just begins to pull away from the side of the bowl. Scrape the dough into the pan and use your hands or a spatula to press it out into an even layer. Bake until the dough is dry but not browned, 10–12 minutes. Cool slightly.

3. Toss the apples, cinnamon, vanilla, nutmeg, and remaining 2 tablespoons whole-wheat flour and ¼ cup sugar together in a large bowl. Spread the mixture evenly over the crust in the pan. Bake until the apples are tender and the crust is browned, about 40 minutes. Cool and cut into 24 (2-inch) squares.

PER SERVING (1 SQUARE): *106 Cal, 3 g Fat, 2 g Sat Fat, 0 g Trans Fat, 8 mg Chol, 1 mg Sod, 18 g Carb, 2 g Fib, 2 g Prot, 9 mg Calc.*

Smart move

A trip to an apple orchard or farm to pick fruit can help your child develop a positive relationship with food and understand its connection to nature, the seasons, and your local area.

FROM TOP, CLOCKWISE: **Frozen Hot Chocolate**, page 209; **Harvest Apple Squares**, page 206; and **Oatmeal Cookies with Cherries and Almonds**, page 212

Brown Rice Crispy Bars

SERVES 16 | PREP 5 minutes | COOK 5 minutes

2 tablespoons almond butter

½ (10-ounce) bag mini marshmallows (3 cups)

2 cups crisp puffed brown rice cereal

1 cup whole-grain flake cereal

2 tablespoons mini chocolate chips

1. Spray an 8-inch-square baking pan and a rubber spatula with nonstick spray.

2. Place the almond butter in a large saucepan and cook over medium-low heat until softened, about 30 seconds. Add the marshmallows and cook until melted but still lumpy, about 2 minutes. Remove from the heat and immediately use the rubber spatula to stir in the rice cereal, whole-grain cereal, and chocolate chips. Continue stirring until well combined.

3. Scrape the mixture into the pan and use the spatula to press it into an even layer and smooth the top. Refrigerate until the bars are firm, about 30 minutes. Use a heavy, sharp knife to cut the mixture into 16 (2-inch) squares.

PER SERVING (1 SQUARE): *68 Cal, 2 g Fat, 0 g Sat Fat, 0 g Trans Fat, 0 mg Chol, 18 mg Sod, 13 g Carb, 1 g Fib, 1 g Prot, 7 mg Calc.*

Try it

We love the way whole grains star in this updated snack classic. If you're concerned about nut allergies, substitute 2 tablespoons unsalted butter for the almond butter.

Frozen Hot Chocolate

SERVES 4 | PREP 5 minutes | COOK 5 minutes

½ cup sugar

¼ cup unsweetened cocoa powder

Pinch salt

2 cups low-fat (1%) milk

1½ teaspoons vanilla extract

1 cup fresh raspberries

1. Combine the sugar, cocoa powder, and salt in a medium saucepan. Slowly whisk in the milk, whisking until smooth. Place the saucepan over medium-high heat and cook, stirring often, until the mixture just simmers, about 5 minutes. Remove from the heat, stir in the vanilla, and pour the mixture into a 9 × 13-inch metal baking pan. Place the pan in the freezer for 30 minutes.

2. Remove the pan from the freezer and use a fork to stir the mixture, breaking up any ice crystals that have formed on the bottom or sides of the pan. Return the pan to the freezer. Repeat the stirring process every 20–30 minutes until the mixture is completely frozen, 3–4 hours. Fluff with a fork, divide between 4 bowls, and serve topped with the raspberries.

PER SERVING (⅔ CUP FROZEN CHOCOLATE AND ¼ CUP RASPBERRIES): *179 Cal, 2 g Fat, 1 g Sat Fat, 0 g Trans Fat, 5 mg Chol, 64 mg Sod, 37 g Carb, 4 g Fib, 5 g Prot, 164 mg Calc.*

Smart move

Enjoying an ice cream cone on a summer afternoon or eating cotton candy at a carnival are some of life's simple pleasures, and they're ones most parents want their kids to have. If you find yourself obsessing over every single food choice your family makes, try to see the bigger picture: As long as the majority of foods they eat are healthful ones, your children will thrive.

Watermelon Cake with Raspberry Sauce

SERVES 16 | PREP 30 minutes | NO COOK

½ seedless watermelon

1 small cantaloupe, halved and seeded

3 kiwi fruits, peeled and sliced

1 pint blueberries

1 pint strawberries, hulled and halved

1½ cups frozen unsweetened raspberries, thawed

3 tablespoons orange juice

2 tablespoons sugar

1. Cut the watermelon into round slices, each about 1½ inches thick. Cut off the rind. Stack the watermelon circles on a large serving platter so that they resemble a cake.

2. Use a melon baller to scoop out balls from the cantaloupe. Decorate the top of the watermelon cake and the plate around it with cantaloupe balls, kiwi slices, blueberries, and strawberries.

3. Combine the raspberries, orange juice, and sugar in a blender and pulse until smooth. Pour the mixture into a fine strainer set over a bowl. Use a spoon to press the sauce through the holes in the strainer. Discard the raspberry seeds.

4. To serve, cut the watermelon cake into wedges and serve with a few spoons of fruit and a drizzle of raspberry sauce.

PER SERVING (1½ CUPS FRUIT AND 1 TABLESPOON SAUCE): *83 Cal, 1 g Fat, 0 g Sat Fat, 0 g Trans Fat, 0 mg Chol, 7 mg Sod, 19 g Carb, 2 g Fib, 2 g Prot, 20 mg Calc.*

Smart move

Keep at least one kind of fruit, washed and cut up, in a clear storage container in the fridge where kids can see it and grab it. Choose fruit that doesn't brown with exposure to oxygen, such as berries, citrus fruits, melons, or pineapple.

Oatmeal Cookies with Cherries and Almonds

SERVES 32 | PREP 15 minutes | BAKE 15 minutes

6 tablespoons unsalted butter, softened

1 cup sugar

1 large egg, at room temperature

1 tablespoon molasses

1 teaspoon vanilla extract

½ teaspoon salt

1½ cups old-fashioned rolled oats

1¼ cups all-purpose flour

¼ cup toasted wheat germ

1 teaspoon baking powder

1 teaspoon cinnamon

½ cup dried cherries

½ cup sliced almonds

1. Arrange racks in the upper and lower thirds of the oven. Preheat the oven to 350°F. Line two baking sheets with parchment paper.

2. Cream the butter and sugar together in the bowl of an electric mixer until fluffy, about 2 minutes on Medium speed. Beat in the egg, molasses, vanilla, and salt. On Low speed, beat in the oats, flour, wheat germ, baking powder, and cinnamon, beating just until the ingredients are combined. Fold in the cherries and almonds.

3. Lightly flour your hands. Take a heaping tablespoon of the dough and roll it into a ball. Repeat, placing the balls on the baking sheets, leaving 2 inches between each. Bake until golden brown, 14–16 minutes. Cool the cookies on the baking sheets for 1 minute, then transfer to a wire rack to cool completely.

PER SERVING (1 COOKIE): *98 Cal, 3 g Fat, 2 g Sat Fat, 0 g Trans Fat, 12 mg Chol, 51 mg Sod, 15 g Carb, 1 g Fib, 2 g Prot, 14 mg Calc.*

Try it

Almonds are high in calcium and fiber, but if you have concerns about nut allergies, substitute ½ cup of dried blueberries or chopped dried apricots.

Caramelized Pears
with Pecans

SERVES 4 | PREP 10 minutes | BAKE 45 minutes

4 large Bartlett pears, peeled, cored, and halved

¼ cup packed light brown sugar

¼ cup chopped pecans

2 tablespoons dried cranberries, coarsely chopped

1. Preheat the oven to 350ºF. Spray a 9 × 13-inch baking pan with nonstick spray.

2. Place the pears, cut side up, in a single layer in the pan. Toss the sugar, pecans, and cranberries together in a small bowl. Spoon the mixture evenly into the pears. Bake until the pears are easily pierced with a knife, about 45 minutes.

PER SERVING (1 PEAR): *191 Cal, 6 g Fat, 1 g Sat Fat, 0 g Trans Fat, 0 mg Chol, 11 mg Sod, 37 g Carb, 3 g Fib, 1 g Prot, 31 mg Calc.*

Kids can...

Place the pear halves in the prepared pan and spoon the brown sugar mixture over the halves.

Frozen Fruit Pops ☺

SERVES 6 | PREP 5 minutes | NO COOK

1 cup unsweetened applesauce

½ cup blueberries

1 (10-ounce) bag frozen cherries, thawed

2 tablespoons orange juice concentrate, thawed

1. Stir the applesauce, blueberries, cherries, and orange juice concentrate together in a medium bowl. Spoon the mixture carefully into 6 ice pop molds and cover with the tops.

2. Freeze the molds until they are solid, at least 4 hours. When ready to serve, let them sit at room temperature for 15 minutes before unmolding.

PER SERVING (1 ICE POP): *66 Cal, 0 g Fat, 0 g Sat Fat, 0 g Trans Fat, 0 mg Chol, 2 mg Sod, 17 g Carb, 1 g Fib, 1 g Prot, 9 mg Calc.*

Kids can...

Stir all the ingredients together with a rubber spatula, then help spoon the mixture into the ice pop molds.

Pomegranate Granita

2 cups pomegranate juice

1 tablespoon lime juice

1 tablespoon honey

1. Stir the pomegranate juice, lime juice, and honey together in a 9 × 13-inch metal baking pan. Place in the freezer for 30 minutes.

2. Remove the pan from the freezer and use a fork to stir the mixture, breaking up any ice crystals that have formed on the bottom or sides of the pan. Return the pan to the freezer. Repeat the stirring process every 30 minutes until the mixture is completely frozen, 3–4 hours. Fluff with a fork, divide among bowls, and serve immediately, or transfer to an airtight container and freeze.

PER SERVING (¾ CUP): *97 Cal, 0 g Fat, 0 g Sat Fat, 0 g Trans Fat, 0 mg Chol, 5 mg Sod, 25 g Carb, 0 g Fib, 0 g Prot, 1 mg Calc.*

Try it

Want a healthful alternative to soda? Mix a favorite juice (such as leftover pomegranate juice from this recipe) with seltzer or club soda. It'll be fizzy and delicious, without as much sugar as most sodas contain.

Carrot Cupcakes with Cream Cheese Frosting

SERVES 12 | PREP 20 minutes | BAKE 25 minutes

1¼ cups all-purpose flour

⅔ cup granulated sugar

2 medium carrots, shredded

1 apple, peeled, cored, and shredded

⅓ cup golden raisins

¼ cup sweetened flaked coconut

1 teaspoon grated orange zest

1 teaspoon cinnamon

1 teaspoon baking soda

¼ teaspoon salt

2 large eggs, lightly beaten

¼ cup canola oil

6 ounces fat-free cream cheese, at room temperature

¼ cup confectioners' sugar, sifted

1 teaspoon vanilla extract

1 tablespoon milk

Mixed candied fruits for decorating tops (optional)

1. Preheat the oven to 350°F. Spray a 12-cup muffin pan with nonstick spray.

2. Stir the flour, granulated sugar, carrots, apple, raisins, coconut, orange zest, cinnamon, baking soda, and salt together in a large bowl. Beat the eggs and oil together in another bowl. Stir the egg mixture into the flour mixture just until combined. Spoon the batter evenly into the muffin cups and bake until a toothpick inserted into the center of each cupcake comes out clean, 20–25 minutes. Cool in the pan on a rack 5 minutes; remove the cupcakes from the pan and cool completely on the rack.

3. To make the frosting, combine the cream cheese, confectioners' sugar, vanilla, and milk in the bowl of an electric mixer and beat just until creamy. Spread the frosting over the cooled cupcakes. Make faces or designs on top of the cupcakes with the dried fruit, if using.

PER SERVING (1 FROSTED CUPCAKE): *202 Cal, 6 g Fat, 1 g Sat Fat, 0 g Trans Fat, 38 mg Chol, 262 mg Sod, 32 g Carb, 1 g Fib, 5 g Prot, 81 mg Calc.*

dry and liquid measurements

If you are converting the recipes in this book to metric measurements or seeking measurement equivalents, use the following charts as a guide.

TEASPOONS	TABLESPOONS	CUPS	FLUID OUNCES
3 teaspoons	1 tablespoon		½ fluid ounce
6 teaspoons	2 tablespoons	⅛ cup	1 fluid ounce
8 teaspoons	2 tablespoons plus 2 teaspoons	⅙ cup	
12 teaspoons	4 tablespoons	¼ cup	2 fluid ounces
15 teaspoons	5 tablespoons	⅓ cup minus 1 teaspoon	
16 teaspoons	5 tablespoons plus 1 teaspoon	⅓ cup	
18 teaspoons	6 tablespoons	¼ cup plus 2 tablespoons	3 fluid ounces
24 teaspoons	8 tablespoons	½ cup	4 fluid ounces
30 teaspoons	10 tablespoons	½ cup plus 2 tablespoons	5 fluid ounces
32 teaspoons	10 tablespoons plus 2 teaspoons	⅔ cup	
36 teaspoons	12 tablespoons	¾ cup	6 fluid ounces
42 teaspoons	14 tablespoons	1 cup minus 2 tablespoons	7 fluid ounces
45 teaspoons	15 tablespoons	1 cup minus 1 tablespoon	
48 teaspoons	16 tablespoons	1 cup	8 fluid ounces

LENGTH

1 inch	25 millimeters
1 inch	2.5 centimeters

OVEN TEMPERATURE

250°F	120°C
275°F	140°C
300°F	150°C
325°F	160°C
350°F	180°C
375°F	190°C
400°F	200°C
425°F	220°C
450°F	230°C
475°F	250°C
500°F	260°C
525°F	270°C

WEIGHT

1 ounce	30 grams
¼ pound	120 grams
½ pound	240 grams
1 pound	480 grams

VOLUME

¼ teaspoon	1 milliliter
½ teaspoon	2 milliliters
1 teaspoon	5 milliliters
1 tablespoon	15 milliliters
2 tablespoons	30 milliliters
3 tablespoons	45 milliliters
¼ cup	60 milliliters
⅓ cup	80 milliliters
½ cup	120 milliliters
⅔ cup	160 milliliters
¾ cup	175 milliliters
1 cup	240 milliliters
1 quart	950 milliliters

NOTE: Measurement of less than ⅛ teaspoon is considered a dash or a pinch. Metric measurements are approximate.

INDEX

F

G

H

S

RECIPE INDEX BY *POINTS* VALUE

5 POINTS value

Braised Bok Choy and Chicken with
    Soba Noodles, 163
Brunch Strata, 106
Chicken in Coconut Curry Sauce, 159
Cuban Picadillo, 150
Grilled Cheese Triangles, 142
Indian-Spiced Lentils, 189
Island Ginger Beef Stew, 144
Lunch Wrap Spirals, 135
Mini Fishwiches, 172
Mushroom Lasagna, 187
Pumpkin Pie Muffins, 115
Shrimp with Cherry Tomatoes and
    Feta, 179
Slow-Cooker Paella with Chicken
    Sausage, 165
Stoplight Pita Sandwiches, 134
Tuna and Shells Salad, 129
Turkey Tabbouleh, 167

6 POINTS value

Black Bean Soup with Rice, 138
Confetti Orzo with Ham and
    Vegetables, 155

Crumb-Topped Mac 'n' Cheese, 192
Fish Tacos with Mango Salsa, 175
Fusilli with Broccoli, Beans, and
    Walnuts, 184
Ham and Turkey Stromboli, 153
Hummus Heads, 133
Oatmeal Pancakes with Blueberry-
    Maple Syrup, 112
Sesame Noodles with Green
    Vegetables, 193
Shrimp and Sausage Jambalaya, 178
Spaghetti Pie, 190
Sushi Shrimp Rolls, 180
Tangy Slow-Cooker Pulled
    Brisket, 146
Vegetable Fried Rice, 183

7 POINTS value

Personal Pizzas, 195
Philly Cheese Steaks, 148
Slow-Cooker Greek Chicken Stew, 164
Slow-Cooker Pork Loin with Apricot
    Glaze, 154